The Giant Book of Unexpected Facts

by
Jake Jacobs

* * * * *

Published by Jake Jacobs

1.

First Presbyterian Church is a term used to refer to the first Presbyterian church established in a particular location.

2.

The first Presbyterian church in the United States was First Presbyterian Church of Philadelphia, founded in 1698.

3.

Many First Presbyterian Churches in the U.S. were established in the 18th and 19th centuries, often during the time of colonial settlement and westward expansion.

4.

The oldest continuously active First Presbyterian Church is believed to be First Presbyterian Church of Hempstead, established in 1659 in New York.

5.

First Presbyterian Churches are found in many cities and towns across the United States, and their architecture often reflects the historical periods in which they were built.

6.

Some First Presbyterian Churches are known for their historic significance, having played roles in the American Revolution or other key historical events.

7.

Many First Presbyterian Churches have beautiful stained glass windows and intricate woodwork, showcasing the craftsmanship of earlier times.

8.

First Presbyterian Churches are often known for their strong sense of community and outreach programs.

9.

Theology and worship styles may vary among First Presbyterian Churches, but they generally adhere to Reformed or Calvinist traditions.

10.

Some First Presbyterian Churches have large pipe organs and choirs that enrich their worship services.

11.

First Presbyterian Churches have been influential in establishing educational institutions, such as colleges and seminaries.

12.

Many First Presbyterian Churches have historic cemeteries where notable figures from the local community are buried.

13.

First Presbyterian Churches have faced challenges over the years, including religious schisms and controversies.

14.

Some First Presbyterian Churches have beautiful gardens or courtyards that provide peaceful spaces for reflection.

15.

The First Presbyterian Church in the United States was organized by Francis Makemie, known as the father of American Presbyterianism.

16.

The First Presbyterian Church of San Francisco, established in 1849, is the oldest Protestant congregation in the city.

17.

First Presbyterian Churches have often been at the forefront of social justice movements, advocating for civil rights and other causes.

18.

First Presbyterian Churches may be affiliated with various Presbyterian denominations, such as the PC(USA), PCA, EPC, and others.

19.

Some First Presbyterian Churches have historic bells that still ring on special occasions.

20.

First Presbyterian Churches have had a significant impact on the cultural and religious landscape of their communities.

21.

The First Presbyterian Church of Bethlehem, Pennsylvania, was founded in 1744 and is one of the oldest continuously operating Presbyterian churches in the U.S.

22.

Some First Presbyterian Churches have notable pipe organs that are considered works of art.

23.

The First Presbyterian Church of Detroit, founded in 1824, is the oldest continuously operating Protestant church in Michigan.

24.

First Presbyterian Churches often have vibrant youth and children's ministries.

25.

Some First Presbyterian Churches have archives and historical collections that preserve their rich heritage.

26.

The First Presbyterian Church of New York City, founded in 1716, is one of the oldest congregations in the city.

27.

First Presbyterian Churches may have beautiful stained glass windows depicting biblical scenes or historical events.

28.

The First Presbyterian Church of Nashville, Tennessee, founded in 1814, played a significant role during the Civil War as a hospital and refuge.

29.

First Presbyterian Churches have been instrumental in providing disaster relief and aid during times of crisis.

30.

Some First Presbyterian Churches have impressive pipe organs with hundreds of pipes.

31.

The First Presbyterian Church of Springfield, Illinois, was attended by Abraham Lincoln and his family during his time as a lawyer and politician.

32.

First Presbyterian Churches may have unique architectural features that set them apart from other churches in their area.

33.

The First Presbyterian Church of Honolulu, Hawaii, founded in 1820, is the oldest congregation in the state.

34.

Some First Presbyterian Churches have beautiful handcrafted wooden pews that have been in use for generations.

35.

First Presbyterian Churches often have vibrant music ministries with choirs and worship bands.

36.

The First Presbyterian Church of Charleston, South Carolina, founded in 1731, is the oldest Presbyterian congregation in the South.

37.

First Presbyterian Churches may offer community outreach programs, such as food banks and homeless shelters.

38.

Some First Presbyterian Churches have historic cemetery plots where notable figures from the church's history are buried.

39.

The First Presbyterian Church of Annapolis, Maryland, founded in 1696, is the oldest Presbyterian congregation in the state.

40.

First Presbyterian Churches have been involved in supporting
missionary efforts both locally and internationally.

41.

The First Presbyterian Church of Albany, New York, founded in
1642, is the second-oldest continuously operating Presbyterian
church in the U.S.

42.

Some First Presbyterian Churches have been recognized as historical
landmarks by local or national preservation organizations.

43.

First Presbyterian Churches have strong ties to their communities
and often host community events and gatherings.

44.

The First Presbyterian Church of Carlisle, Pennsylvania, founded in
1734, is one of the oldest Presbyterian congregations in the country.

45.

Some First Presbyterian Churches have unique handcrafted stained
glass windows designed by renowned artists.

46.

First Presbyterian Churches often have active Sunday School
programs and educational opportunities for all ages.

47.

The First Presbyterian Church of Stamford, Connecticut, founded in
1642, is the third-oldest continuously operating Presbyterian church
in the U.S.

48.

Some First Presbyterian Churches have beautiful pipe organs with intricate wood carvings.

49.

First Presbyterian Churches have been instrumental in supporting educational institutions, such as seminaries and schools.

50.

The First Presbyterian Church of Albuquerque, New Mexico, founded in 1881, is the oldest Protestant church in the city.

51.

Fort Shantok Archeological District is a historical site located in Uncasville, Connecticut, USA.

52.

The district is situated on the east bank of the Thames River and covers an area of approximately 43 acres.

53.

Fort Shantok was originally an ancient Mohegan Native American village that dates back to the 1600s.

54.

The Mohegan tribe inhabited the area for centuries before European settlers arrived in the region.

55.

The name "Shantok" is derived from the Mohegan word "chintock," meaning "place of the big mountain."

56.

The site was strategically located along the Thames River, providing access to trade and transportation routes.

57.

The district was added to the National Register of Historic Places in 1984.

58.

Fort Shantok was a significant settlement during the Pequot War of 1637, a conflict between English colonists and the Pequot and Mohegan tribes.

59.

The fort served as a stronghold for the Mohegan tribe during the war, providing a defensive advantage.

60.

The Mohegan leader Uncas played a pivotal role in the history of Fort Shantok. He was a key ally to the English during the Pequot War.

61.

Archaeological excavations at the site have revealed artifacts and remnants of the Mohegan village and fortifications.

62.

The district includes the remnants of wigwam platforms and post molds, providing insights into the construction of Mohegan dwellings.

63.

The area surrounding Fort Shantok was historically abundant in natural resources, making it an ideal location for settlement.

64.

The fort's strategic location allowed the Mohegan people to engage in trade with neighboring tribes and European settlers.

65.

In 1637, Fort Shantok became a refuge for Mohegan and Pequot people fleeing from English forces during the Pequot War.

66.

The site was also a gathering place for Native American councils and ceremonies.

67.

Fort Shantok Archeological District is managed by the Connecticut Department of Energy and Environmental Protection.

68.

Visitors to the district can explore interpretive trails that provide historical information about the site and the Mohegan people.

69.

The Mohegan Tribe still considers Fort Shantok a sacred and culturally significant place.

70.

The district offers a glimpse into the daily life, customs, and traditions of the Mohegan people who once inhabited the area.

71.

Archaeological studies have revealed evidence of prehistoric Native American occupation at Fort Shantok dating back thousands of years.

72.

The site has been the subject of archaeological research since the 1950s, leading to a better understanding of the region's indigenous history.

73.

Fort Shantok Archeological District is one of the few preserved Native American archaeological sites in Connecticut.

74.

The district is an important cultural resource for the Mohegan Tribe, as it allows them to connect with their ancestral heritage.

75.

Mohegan Sun, one of the largest and most famous casinos in the United States, is located adjacent to Fort Shantok.

76.

The Mohegan Tribe, descendants of the original inhabitants of Fort Shantok, now operates the Mohegan Sun Casino.

77.

The Mohegan Tribe is one of two federally recognized tribes in Connecticut, the other being the Mashantucket Pequot Tribe.

78.

Fort Shantok Archeological District is an important site for understanding the early interactions between Native Americans and European settlers.

79.

The district's inclusion on the National Register of Historic Places ensures its preservation and protection.

80.

Fort Shantok is believed to have been occupied by the Mohegan people until the late 17th century.

81.

The Mohegan Tribe has a rich cultural heritage, and their traditional practices and ceremonies continue to be an integral part of their identity.

82.

The Fort Shantok site has been used for educational programs and cultural events, allowing visitors to learn about the history of the Mohegan people.

83.

The area surrounding Fort Shantok is now a mix of woodland and open space, providing a natural setting for exploration.

84.

The district is open to the public, and visitors are encouraged to respect the cultural significance of the site.

85.

The preservation of Fort Shantok Archeological District serves as a testament to the importance of protecting Native American heritage.

86.

The Mohegan Tribe operates the Tantaquidgeon Indian Museum, which showcases the history and culture of the Mohegan people.

87.

The museum, located nearby, offers exhibits and programs that provide insight into Mohegan traditions and contemporary life.

88.

Fort Shantok Archeological District is a designated State Archaeological Preserve, emphasizing its significance as a historical and cultural site.

89.

The Mohegan Tribe has actively participated in the preservation and interpretation of Fort Shantok, sharing their knowledge and insights with visitors.

90.

Fort Shantok and the Mohegan Tribe's history are closely tied to the broader context of Native American interactions with European colonists.

91.

The district's significance extends beyond its archaeological value, serving as a living reminder of the enduring Mohegan culture.

92.

The Fort Shantok site is situated on land that is part of the Mohegan Indian Reservation.

93.

Fort Shantok Archeological District showcases the resilience and adaptability of the Mohegan people over centuries of cultural change.

94.

The Mohegan Tribe continues to be actively involved in archaeological research and cultural preservation efforts at Fort Shantok.

95.

The district's significance as a cultural heritage site has attracted scholars and researchers from various disciplines.

96.

The Mohegan Tribe's history includes a strong tradition of storytelling, which has been instrumental in passing down their cultural knowledge.

97.

The Mohegan Tribe's government and cultural programs work to ensure the preservation of their traditions and language for future generations.

98.

The Mohegan Tribe's annual Wigwam Festival is held near Fort Shantok and provides an opportunity to celebrate and share their culture.

99.

Fort Shantok Archeological District is a unique site that offers a window into the rich cultural heritage of the Mohegan people.

100.

The district's historical significance and connection to the Mohegan Tribe make it a vital part of Connecticut's cultural heritage and a place of reflection on the history of indigenous peoples in the region.

101.

Greater spot-nosed monkeys, also known as putty-nosed monkeys, are medium-sized primates belonging to the Cercopithecidae family.

102.

They are found in the tropical rainforests of West and Central Africa, including countries like Nigeria, Cameroon, Gabon, and the Republic of the Congo.

103.

Greater spot-nosed monkeys have a distinctive appearance with dark fur, a white nose spot, and white patches on their cheeks.

104.

These monkeys are highly social animals and live in groups, called troops, consisting of several individuals.

105.

Troops of greater spot-nosed monkeys are led by a dominant male, and they have a complex social hierarchy.

106.

Female spot-nosed monkeys play a significant role in the troop's social structure and are responsible for grooming and caring for the young.

107.

Spot-nosed monkeys are diurnal, which means they are active during the day and rest at night.

108.

They are omnivorous and have a varied diet that includes fruits, leaves, insects, and small vertebrates.

109.

Greater spot-nosed monkeys use different vocalizations, including whistles, grunts, and barks, to communicate with each other and alert the troop about potential dangers.

110.

These monkeys are agile climbers and spend a significant amount of time in the treetops, where they search for food and escape predators.

111.

They have excellent eyesight and a well-developed sense of smell, which helps them locate food and identify predators.

112.

Greater spot-nosed monkeys have a gestation period of around five to six months, and females usually give birth to a single offspring.

113.

The mother carries the newborn on her belly for the first few weeks, and then it will be gradually allowed to explore its surroundings.

114.

Spot-nosed monkeys face threats from habitat loss due to deforestation and illegal hunting for bushmeat.

115.

They are listed as near-threatened on the IUCN Red List of Threatened Species due to their declining populations.

116.

Spot-nosed monkeys have been studied extensively by primatologists, contributing valuable insights into primate behavior and social dynamics.

117.

The white patches on their cheeks are believed to serve as a form of visual communication, especially during social interactions.

118.

Spot-nosed monkeys groom each other regularly, which helps in maintaining social bonds within the troop.

119.

They have specialized cheek pouches that allow them to store food while foraging, which they consume later when safe.

120.

Greater spot-nosed monkeys are known for their acrobatic skills, often leaping from branch to branch with agility.

121.

These monkeys are very curious creatures and often investigate their environment to find new food sources and opportunities.

122.

Spot-nosed monkeys play a crucial role in seed dispersal, helping to regenerate the forest by spreading seeds to different areas.

123.

They have well-developed thumbs, which enables them to grasp and manipulate objects with precision.

124.

Spot-nosed monkeys have a specialized stomach that helps them digest fibrous plant material effectively.

125.

They are highly adaptable and can survive in a wide range of forest habitats, including primary and secondary forests.

126.

Spot-nosed monkeys are highly vocal during social encounters and can produce a wide range of vocalizations to convey different messages.

127.

They have a unique way of yawning with their jaws wide open, which is believed to be a communication gesture.

128.

The white nose spot of these monkeys stands out against their dark fur, making it easier for group members to identify each other.

129.

Spot-nosed monkeys use a variety of facial expressions, body postures, and vocalizations to express emotions and intentions.

130.

Their long, slender fingers and toes provide excellent grip and dexterity when navigating through the forest canopy.

131.

Spot-nosed monkeys are known to display affiliative behaviors, such as hugging and embracing each other, as a way of strengthening social bonds.

132.

In some cultures, spot-nosed monkeys are considered sacred animals and are protected by local communities.

133.

They are highly alert to their surroundings and can quickly respond to potential threats by taking refuge in the treetops.

134.

Spot-nosed monkeys have a high-pitched alarm call that alerts the entire troop about potential predators.

135.

They often engage in play activities, such as chasing each other, swinging from branches, and engaging in mock fights.

136.

In some areas, greater spot-nosed monkeys have been observed using tools, such as leaves or sticks, to extract insects from tree bark.

137.

They are known to form multi-male, multi-female social groups that allow for multiple breeding opportunities for dominant males.

138.

Spot-nosed monkeys are adept at using their tails for balance while leaping and climbing through the forest canopy.

139.

Their fur color can vary between subspecies, with some individuals having a more reddish hue and others having a darker brown coloration.

140.

Spot-nosed monkeys exhibit a unique behavior known as "pillar-sitting," where they sit upright on tree branches, resembling pillars.

141.

In addition to vocalizations, spot-nosed monkeys use body language, such as raised hair and tail movements, to communicate emotions.

142.

They have a strong preference for fruits and will actively search for ripe fruits in the canopy.

143.

Greater spot-nosed monkeys have been observed using leaves as makeshift umbrellas to shield themselves from rain.

144.

Spot-nosed monkeys are highly territorial and will defend their territories from other troops.

145.

They are known to engage in territorial displays, such as raising their fur and vocalizing loudly to intimidate intruders.

146.

Spot-nosed monkeys have a keen sense of spatial memory, allowing them to navigate through their home range efficiently.

147.

They are excellent swimmers and are capable of crossing rivers and streams when necessary.

148.

Spot-nosed monkeys have been documented engaging in self-directed behaviors, such as scratching and grooming, as a form of self-care.

149.

Greater spot-nosed monkeys play a crucial role in the ecosystem by helping to disperse seeds of various plant species.

150.

These intelligent and social primates continue to captivate researchers and wildlife enthusiasts, providing valuable insights into the complex world of primates in the African rainforests.

151.

Green caterpillars are the larval stage of various species of butterflies and moths, characterized by their green coloration.

152.

The green color of the caterpillar acts as a form of camouflage, helping them blend in with the surrounding foliage and protect them from predators.

153.

Green caterpillars are herbivorous and primarily feed on leaves, although some species may eat flowers or other plant parts.

154.

The green coloration is due to the presence of chlorophyll in their bodies, which helps them process sunlight and convert it into energy.

155.

Caterpillars have six true legs and several pairs of fleshy prolegs, which aid in their movement and grip on surfaces.

156.

Many species of green caterpillars have distinctive markings or patterns on their bodies, making them visually appealing and unique.

157.

Some green caterpillars have spines or bristles as a defense mechanism against predators, causing irritation or discomfort upon contact.

158.

Caterpillars go through a series of molts, shedding their exoskeletons as they grow and increase in size.

159.

The process of metamorphosis transforms the caterpillar into a chrysalis or pupa, from which the adult butterfly or moth eventually emerges.

160.

Green caterpillars play an essential role in the ecosystem by consuming plant matter and converting it into energy, which is then transferred through the food chain.

161.

The caterpillar's body is divided into distinct segments, each with specialized functions.

162.

Some green caterpillars are known for their unique behaviors, such as creating silk threads to move between branches or leaves.

163.

The length of the caterpillar's life stage can vary greatly, ranging from a few weeks to several months, depending on the species and environmental conditions.

164.

The green coloration of caterpillars can change slightly based on their diet and environmental factors.

165.

Some species of green caterpillars are considered pests to agricultural crops, as they can cause significant damage to plants.

166.

Green caterpillars have several natural enemies, including birds, insects, and spiders, which feed on them during their vulnerable larval stage.

167.

The caterpillar's primary goal is to eat and grow, consuming vast amounts of food to fuel its metamorphosis into an adult.

168.

Some green caterpillars have evolved unique defense mechanisms, such as emitting strong odors or toxins to deter predators.

169.

Caterpillars have specialized mouthparts, known as mandibles, which they use to chew and consume plant material.

170.

The silk produced by caterpillars is primarily used to create cocoons or shelters during their pupal stage.

171.

Some green caterpillars have fascinating patterns or eye-like markings on their bodies, which may help scare away potential predators.

172.

Caterpillars have a soft, cylindrical body, making them flexible and able to navigate through narrow spaces.

173.

The size of a caterpillar can range from a few millimeters to several inches, depending on the species.

174.

Some species of green caterpillars are migratory and travel long distances in search of food or suitable breeding grounds.

175.

Caterpillars can engage in mimicry, imitating the appearance of other insects or objects to avoid detection by predators.

176.

Some green caterpillars are known for their ability to drop from trees or plants when threatened, using silk threads as a safety line.

177.

Certain species of green caterpillars display bright warning colors or aposematic patterns to indicate their toxicity or unpalatability to predators.

178.

Green caterpillars have a voracious appetite and can consume several times their body weight in plant material each day.

179.

Some green caterpillars are nocturnal, feeding primarily during the nighttime and resting during the day.

180.

The transformation from a caterpillar to a butterfly or moth is one of the most remarkable examples of biological metamorphosis in the animal kingdom.

181.

Caterpillars communicate with each other through tactile interactions, vibrations, and chemical signals.

182.

Some species of green caterpillars exhibit social behaviors, with multiple individuals living together in communal webs or nests.

183.

Caterpillars play a vital role in pollination as they move from one plant to another in search of food.

184.

Certain species of green caterpillars are used in scientific research to study various biological processes and environmental impacts.

185.

The timing of a caterpillar's metamorphosis is often influenced by factors such as temperature, light, and the availability of food.

186.

Some caterpillar species have evolved cryptic behaviors, such as swaying like a leaf in the wind, to avoid detection by predators.

187.

Green caterpillars undergo a significant change in their body structure during metamorphosis, as they reorganize their tissues to become an adult butterfly or moth.

188.

Some caterpillars produce substances that protect them from predators, such as repellent chemicals or irritants.

189.

The silk produced by caterpillars is incredibly strong, and some species use it to build elaborate nests or shelters for protection.

190.

Caterpillars are essential components of food webs, providing a crucial link between plants and higher-level consumers.

191.

Some caterpillar species have symbiotic relationships with ants, which protect the caterpillars from predators in exchange for sweet secretions.

192.

The study of caterpillars, known as lepidopterology, has led to significant advancements in understanding insect biology and ecology.

193.

Some green caterpillar species have evolved to resemble inedible or poisonous objects, such as bird droppings or thorns.

194.

Caterpillars have specialized cells called imaginal discs, which develop into adult body parts during metamorphosis.

195.

Some caterpillar species migrate to specific locations to find suitable conditions for pupation and hatching.

196.

The silk produced by caterpillars is one of the strongest natural fibers, with incredible tensile strength and durability.

197.

The coloration and pattern of a caterpillar's body can change as it progresses through different instars (stages) during its growth.

198.

Certain species of green caterpillars have developed mutualistic relationships with specific plant species, benefiting both the caterpillar and the plant.

199.

Caterpillars have developed different strategies for avoiding predation, including staying motionless when threatened or rapidly moving to escape.

200.

Green caterpillars are fascinating creatures that provide numerous ecological benefits and have captured the curiosity and interest of scientists, naturalists, and nature enthusiasts worldwide.

201.

The Abbott Company was founded in 1888 by Dr. Wallace C. Abbott in Chicago, Illinois.

202.

It started as a pharmaceutical company specializing in the production of alkaloidal and botanical drugs.

203.

The company's first product was a digestive remedy called "Mistura Abbott," which became widely popular.

204.

Abbott was one of the first companies to produce standardized pharmaceuticals, ensuring consistent quality and potency.

205.

In 1910, Abbott introduced a milk-based infant formula called "Similac," which revolutionized infant nutrition.

206.

During World War II, Abbott played a significant role in producing essential medical supplies for the military.

207.

In the 1950s, Abbott expanded internationally and opened its first overseas subsidiary in Venezuela.

208.

The company's growth continued, and by the 1960s, Abbott had a presence in multiple countries across the globe.

209.

In 1964, Abbott introduced "Pentothal," a widely used anesthetic drug.

210.

In the 1970s, Abbott expanded its portfolio to include medical devices, diagnostics, and nutritional products.

211.

Abbott's acquisition of Ross Laboratories in 1971 solidified its position in the infant nutrition market.

212.

In 1985, Abbott developed the first commercially available HIV blood test, significantly impacting the AIDS epidemic.

213.

The company's medical device division developed the first-ever drug-eluting stent, called "Xience," used to treat coronary artery disease.

214.

Abbott became a leader in the field of diagnostics with the development of advanced testing systems for various medical conditions.

215.

Abbott's acquisition of Knoll Pharmaceuticals in 2001 expanded its pharmaceutical offerings, including key drugs for various therapeutic areas.

216.

In 2007, Abbott acquired the pharmaceutical division of Solvay, strengthening its global pharmaceutical presence.

217.

Abbott launched "Ensure," a popular nutritional supplement for adults, in 1973.

218.

The company's research in virology and vaccine development led to the creation of vaccines for various diseases, including hepatitis A and B.

219.

Abbott established a strong presence in the field of cardiovascular care with drugs like "Tricor" and "Niaspan."

220.

In 2010, Abbott separated its research-based pharmaceutical business and became two independent companies: Abbott, focused on diversified healthcare products, and AbbVie, focused on research-based pharmaceuticals.

221.

Abbott's "FreeStyle Libre" system revolutionized glucose monitoring for people with diabetes by eliminating the need for fingersticks.

222.

The company has been at the forefront of developing COVID-19 testing and diagnostic solutions to combat the pandemic.

223.

Abbott's "Alinity" family of diagnostic instruments offers high-throughput testing capabilities for laboratories worldwide.

224.

Abbott is committed to sustainability and has set ambitious environmental goals, including reducing greenhouse gas emissions and water usage.

225.

The company has a strong focus on corporate social responsibility, supporting numerous community initiatives and philanthropic programs.

226.

Abbott's "MitraClip" device provides a non-surgical option for people with mitral regurgitation, a heart valve disorder.

227.

Abbott's nutrition division offers a wide range of products, including adult nutrition, pediatric nutrition, and sports nutrition.

228.

The company's medical devices include products for cardiovascular care, diabetes management, and neuromodulation.

229.

Abbott's "i-STAT" handheld blood analyzer allows for quick and accurate point-of-care testing.

230.

Abbott has a long history of investing in research and development, leading to numerous groundbreaking medical advancements.

231.

The company has received numerous awards and recognitions for its commitment to innovation and excellence.

232.

Abbott has a strong commitment to diversity and inclusion, with initiatives to promote gender and racial equality in the workplace.

233.

Abbott's global presence spans over 160 countries, with manufacturing facilities and research centers worldwide.

234.

The company collaborates with various healthcare organizations, governments, and non-profit groups to address global health challenges.

235.

Abbott has been listed on the Fortune 500 list of America's largest companies for many years.

236.

The company's core values include a focus on patient-centered care, scientific excellence, and ethical conduct.

237.

Abbott's "Humira" is one of the world's best-selling drugs and is used to treat various autoimmune diseases.

238.

The company is committed to reducing its environmental impact by implementing sustainable practices throughout its operations.

239.

Abbott's "EAS" brand offers a wide range of sports nutrition products for athletes and fitness enthusiasts.

240.

Abbott has a strong commitment to providing access to healthcare in underserved communities through various outreach programs.

241.

The company's "RealTime CGM" system provides continuous glucose monitoring for people with diabetes, helping them manage their condition effectively.

242.

Abbott's "Pedialyte" is a well-known oral rehydration solution for children and adults during illness or dehydration.

243.

Abbott has been recognized as one of the "World's Most Admired Companies" by Fortune magazine.

244.

The company's "BinaxNOW" COVID-19 Ag Card received Emergency Use Authorization from the FDA for rapid testing.

245.

Abbott has a robust pipeline of new products and therapies under development to address unmet medical needs.

246.

The company's "Alinity m" molecular diagnostics system enables high-volume testing for infectious diseases.

247.

Abbott's "Plex-ID" system is capable of identifying multiple pathogens in a single sample, helping with outbreak investigation.

248.

Abbott's "ARCHITECT" clinical chemistry analyzer provides accurate and reliable testing for various medical conditions.

249.

Abbott has received numerous awards for its commitment to workplace diversity and inclusion.

250.

The company's commitment to innovation, research, and patient care continues to drive its success as a leading global healthcare company.

251.

Xerox Corporation, commonly known as Xerox, was founded on April 18, 1906, as The Haloid Photographic Company in Rochester, New York.

252.

The company's initial focus was on producing photographic paper and equipment.

253.

In 1938, Chester Carlson, a physicist, invented the process of electrophotography, which laid the foundation for modern photocopying.

254.

The first successful photocopier using Carlson's technology, called the "Xerox Model A," was produced in 1949.

255.

The term "Xerox" is derived from a combination of "xer-" from "xerography" and "-ox" from "oxford," the name of the original founder's hometown.

256.

In 1959, Xerox introduced the iconic "914," the world's first plain paper photocopier, which revolutionized the office automation industry.

257.

The introduction of the Xerox 914 marked the birth of the modern photocopier industry.

258.

In 1963, Xerox opened its Palo Alto Research Center (PARC), which became a hotbed of innovation, leading to the development of many groundbreaking technologies.

259.

Xerox PARC is credited with inventing the first personal computer (Alto), graphical user interface (GUI), Ethernet, laser printer, and many other influential technologies.

260.

Xerox's Alto computer inspired the development of Apple's Lisa and Macintosh computers.

261.

Xerox introduced the "Xerox 1200," the first commercially successful color photocopier, in 1973.

262.

Xerox faced a major antitrust lawsuit in the 1970s, which led to a significant change in the company's business practices.

263.

In the 1980s, Xerox expanded its product offerings to include office equipment, such as laser printers and fax machines.

264.

The Xerox "Star," introduced in 1981, was the first commercial computer system with a GUI and mouse, years ahead of other systems.

265.

In 1982, Xerox acquired the financial services company Crum & Forster, which later became the foundation of its insurance and financial services division.

266.

During the 1980s and 1990s, Xerox faced stiff competition from other copier and printer manufacturers, leading to financial challenges.

267.

Xerox went through a major restructuring in the late 1990s to focus on its core businesses and improve profitability.

268.

In 2000, Xerox launched the "DocuColor iGen3," the first digital color press, setting new standards for high-quality digital printing.

269.

In 2001, Xerox introduced the "DocuTech," a high-speed digital production printer for the printing industry.

270.

Xerox acquired the Global Imaging Systems in 2007, expanding its presence in the small and mid-sized business market.

271.

Xerox has a strong commitment to environmental sustainability, aiming to reduce its carbon footprint and promote responsible resource use.

272.

In 2010, Xerox acquired Affiliated Computer Services (ACS), a business process outsourcing company, to expand its services portfolio.

273.

Xerox has made significant investments in research and development, leading to the creation of innovative products and technologies.

274.

Xerox's solid ink technology, used in some of its printers, reduces waste and has a lower environmental impact compared to traditional toner-based printing.

275.

Xerox introduced "ConnectKey," a software platform that integrates office equipment with cloud services and mobile devices, enhancing productivity.

276.

The company's "VersaLink" and "AltaLink" series of printers and multifunction devices received numerous industry awards for innovation and design.

277.

Xerox is a pioneer in the development of digital printing and production printing technology.

278.

The company has a long-standing commitment to diversity and inclusion in its workforce.

279.

Xerox is a prominent player in managed print services, helping businesses optimize their printing infrastructure and reduce costs.

280.

The "Xerox ColorQube" series of printers features environmentally friendly solid ink technology and energy-saving features.

281.

Xerox has a strong focus on corporate social responsibility, supporting various community and educational initiatives.

282.

The "Xerox Brenva" and "Xerox Rialto" inkjet production presses are known for their high-speed and cost-efficient printing capabilities.

283.

Xerox's "Eureka" research division focuses on developing cutting-edge technologies and innovative solutions for the future.

284.

In 2020, Xerox announced its "Project Own It," a strategic initiative to drive growth and innovation in its business.

285.

Xerox has a rich legacy of innovation and holds thousands of patents in various fields.

286.

The company's "Iridesse" digital production press allows for printing metallic and specialty colors in a single pass.

287.

Xerox has been recognized for its efforts in reducing greenhouse gas emissions and promoting sustainable business practices.

288.

Xerox's "FreeFlow" software suite streamlines printing workflows, enhancing efficiency and productivity.

289.

Xerox has a strong commitment to data security and offers secure printing solutions to protect sensitive information.

290.

The company's "XMPie" software enables personalized and variable data printing, empowering marketers to create customized print materials.

291.

Xerox has a global presence, serving customers in over 160 countries.

292.

The company's "Baltoro" inkjet press combines high-quality output with automated features for efficient production printing.

293.

Xerox invests in programs to promote science, technology, engineering, and math (STEM) education for students.

294.

Xerox's "DocuShare" content management platform allows businesses to securely store, manage, and share documents electronically.

295.

The company's "Xerox PrimeLink" series offers advanced production capabilities and exceptional image quality.

296.

Xerox continues to evolve its services and solutions to meet the changing needs of the digital workplace.

297.

The company's "Xerox Adaptive CMYK Plus Technology" allows for printing vibrant colors and specialty enhancements.

298.

Xerox has received numerous accolades for its commitment to innovation and sustainability.

299.

The company actively supports diversity in the printing and graphic communications industry through various initiatives.

300.

Xerox continues to be a leader in the digital printing industry, driving advancements and delivering innovative solutions for businesses worldwide.

301.

The Florence Griswold House and Museum is located in Old Lyme, Connecticut, and is listed on the National Register of Historic Places.

302.

The house was originally built in 1817 as a family home for William Noyes, a prominent sea captain.

303.

In 1899, the house was purchased by Florence Griswold, who turned it into an artist colony known as the Lyme Art Colony.

304.

The Lyme Art Colony was one of the most famous art colonies in America during the late 19th and early 20th centuries.

305.

Notable artists such as Childe Hassam, Willard Metcalf, and Henry Ward Ranger were among the many who stayed and worked at the Florence Griswold House.

306.

The artists who lived and worked at the colony were collectively known as the "Griswold Girls" or "American Impressionists."

307.

The house is situated on the banks of the Lieutenant River, providing a scenic and tranquil setting that inspired many of the artists' works.

308.

Florence Griswold's home became known as the "Florence Griswold House" and was the heart of the Lyme Art Colony.

309.

The walls of the house are adorned with painted panels created by the resident artists, making it a unique and artistically rich space.

310.

The dining room of the house, known as the "Magic Room," features a mural painted by Henry Ward Ranger and other artists, depicting an enchanted woodland scene.

311.

The house and its gardens have been restored to reflect the appearance of the Lyme Art Colony's heyday in the early 20th century.

312.

In addition to the Florence Griswold House, the museum also includes an exhibition gallery showcasing American art from the 18th to the 20th centuries.

313.

The museum's collection includes works by the Lyme Art Colony artists, as well as other American artists such as John Frederick Kensett and William Merritt Chase.

314.

The museum's Krieble Gallery hosts rotating exhibitions of contemporary artists and thematic shows related to American art.

315.

The Florence Griswold House and Museum is known for its picturesque gardens, which have been meticulously restored to resemble the gardens during the Lyme Art Colony era.

316.

The museum organizes various events and programs, including art classes, concerts, and educational activities for children and adults.

317.

Each year, the museum holds an outdoor event called "Wee Faerie Village," where artists create miniature fairy houses in the gardens.

318.

The Florence Griswold House and Museum hosts an annual "Paint-Out Weekend," where contemporary artists gather to paint on the museum grounds, continuing the artistic tradition of the Lyme Art Colony.

319.

The museum's gift shop offers a wide range of art-related items, including books, prints, and artisan crafts.

320.

The house was designated a National Historic Landmark in 1993 in recognition of its significance in American art history.

321.

The museum's collection has grown over the years through donations and acquisitions, making it a valuable resource for American art enthusiasts and researchers.

322.

The Lyme Art Association, founded in 1914, is still active today and holds regular exhibitions at the museum.

323.

The Florence Griswold House and Museum is a popular destination for art lovers, history enthusiasts, and families exploring the Connecticut shoreline.

324.

The museum collaborates with other institutions and art organizations to promote the legacy of the Lyme Art Colony and American Impressionism.

325.

The museum's archives contain a wealth of historical documents, photographs, and letters related to the Lyme Art Colony and its artists.

326.

In 2000, the museum acquired the collection of the Hartford Steam Boiler Inspection and Insurance Company, adding important American artworks to its holdings.

327.

The museum offers guided tours of the Florence Griswold House, providing visitors with insights into the lives and artistic contributions of the Lyme Art Colony artists.

328.

The museum's "Grassy Hill" property features an outdoor installation of sculptures, enhancing the artistic ambiance of the grounds.

329.

The Florence Griswold House and Museum hosts "Artists' Choice" exhibitions, where contemporary artists select artworks from the museum's collection and display them alongside their own creations.

330.

The museum's historical significance extends beyond art, as it also documents the social and cultural life of the Lyme Art Colony and the town of Old Lyme.

331.

The museum's "Cover Stories" exhibit showcases art from the museum's collection that has been featured on magazine covers, illustrating the widespread appeal and recognition of the artists' works.

332.

The museum's archives contain letters written by artists to Florence Griswold, offering glimpses into their artistic processes and personal lives.

333.

The museum has been a leader in promoting American Impressionism and the legacy of the Lyme Art Colony through scholarly research and publications.

334.

The museum's grounds, including the artistically landscaped gardens, provide a serene and idyllic setting for visitors to explore.

335.

The museum's education programs cater to diverse audiences, including school groups, seniors, and families, fostering a greater appreciation for American art and culture.

336.

The museum's "Historic Artists' Homes and Studios" program, a collaboration with other museums, showcases the living and working spaces of renowned American artists.

337.

The Florence Griswold House and Museum's reputation has attracted renowned artists, scholars, and curators to its exhibitions and events.

338.

The museum's annual gala, "The Weir Farm Art Center Benefit," celebrates American art and raises funds to support the museum's initiatives.

339.

The Florence Griswold House and Museum has been featured in various publications and media outlets, furthering its reputation as a center for American art and culture.

340.

The museum's mission includes preserving and sharing the rich artistic heritage of the Lyme Art Colony for future generations.

341.

The Florence Griswold House and Museum actively collaborates with local schools and educational institutions to promote arts education in the community.

342.

The museum's "Art Now" lecture series features presentations by contemporary artists and art experts, offering insights into current trends in American art.

343.

The museum's "On the Porch" concert series showcases musical performances in the picturesque setting of the museum's grounds.

344.

The Florence Griswold House and Museum serves as a cultural hub for the community, hosting events that bring together artists, collectors, and art enthusiasts.

345.

The museum's outreach programs, such as "Art Cart," bring art experiences and activities to schools and community events.

346.

The museum's "Van Gogh Comes to America" exhibition in 1998 explored the influence of Vincent van Gogh's art on American artists and received national acclaim.

347.

The museum's collection of American art includes a diverse range of styles, from Impressionism to modern and contemporary works.

348.

The Florence Griswold House and Museum has played a significant role in fostering a sense of artistic identity in the town of Old Lyme.

349.

The museum's research library contains an extensive collection of books, catalogs, and exhibition materials related to American art and artists.

350.

The Florence Griswold House and Museum continues to be a vibrant center for American art, contributing to the cultural enrichment of the region and promoting the enduring legacy of the Lyme Art Colony.

351.

Grove Street Cemetery is located in New Haven, Connecticut, and is one of the oldest burial grounds in the United States.

352.

The cemetery was established in 1796 and is also known as the New Haven Burying Ground.

353.

It was the first planned cemetery in the United States and served as a model for many later cemeteries across the country.

354.

The cemetery was designed by architect James Hillhouse, who also served as one of its early directors.

355.

Grove Street Cemetery was created as a response to overcrowding in the town's older burial grounds and to provide a more organized and landscaped space for burials.

356.

The cemetery's entrance features a grand Egyptian Revival gateway, which is a notable architectural feature of the site.

357.

Some of the prominent individuals buried at Grove Street Cemetery include Eli Whitney, inventor of the cotton gin; Noah Webster, lexicographer and author of the first American dictionary; and Charles Goodyear, the inventor of vulcanized rubber.

358.

The cemetery is the final resting place for several Yale University presidents and faculty members, including Theodore Dwight Woolsey and Benjamin Silliman.

359.

It is estimated that over 14,000 individuals are buried at Grove Street Cemetery, with over 4,000 monuments and markers.

360.

The cemetery features a wide variety of grave markers and monuments, representing different architectural styles and periods.

361.

The cemetery's central avenue is lined with beautiful mature trees, providing a serene and peaceful atmosphere.

362.

Grove Street Cemetery is often referred to as the "Yale Cemetery" due to its close proximity to Yale University and the large number of Yale-affiliated individuals buried there.

363.

The cemetery has several sections dedicated to different religious denominations, including Congregational, Episcopal, and Catholic sections.

364.

Notable authors, poets, and educators are buried at Grove Street Cemetery, including Lyman Beecher Stowe (brother of Harriet Beecher Stowe) and poet Lydia Sigourney.

365.

The cemetery contains several family plots and mausoleums, showcasing the wealth and status of some of the prominent families buried there.

366.

The cemetery is a popular destination for history enthusiasts, genealogists, and visitors interested in exploring the lives and legacies of early American figures.

367.

In 2000, Grove Street Cemetery was designated as a National Historic Landmark by the U.S. Department of the Interior.

368.

The cemetery is a prime example of the "rural cemetery" movement, which emphasized landscaping and creating a park-like setting for the dead.

369.

The cemetery has inspired numerous poets and writers, including Emily Dickinson, who visited the cemetery and wrote poems about it.

370.

The cemetery's layout and design influenced the development of other rural cemeteries in the United States, such as Mount Auburn Cemetery in Massachusetts.

371.

The cemetery is open to the public for self-guided tours, and guided tours are also offered by volunteers and staff.

372.

The cemetery is known for its beautiful spring bloom when the numerous flowering trees and shrubs create a colorful display.

373.

Many of the grave markers and monuments at Grove Street Cemetery feature intricate carvings and symbols, reflecting the beliefs and sentiments of the era.

374.

Several well-known architects and sculptors designed monuments at the cemetery, making it an outdoor gallery of art and architecture.

375.

The cemetery contains several war memorials and monuments honoring soldiers who served in various conflicts, including the Civil War.

376.

Grove Street Cemetery has been the subject of several historical preservation efforts to maintain and protect its rich history and architectural features.

377.

The cemetery hosts special events and programs throughout the year, including lectures, art exhibitions, and musical performances.

378.

The cemetery is a peaceful retreat in the heart of the city and is a popular spot for local residents to walk, jog, or meditate.

379.

Grove Street Cemetery is a member of the Association for Gravestone Studies, an organization dedicated to the preservation and study of gravestones and burial grounds.

380.

The cemetery was featured in the movie "Amistad," directed by Steven Spielberg, as it was a pivotal location in the historical events depicted in the film.

381.

The cemetery's records and archives are an invaluable resource for historians and genealogists researching the history of New Haven and its residents.

382.

Grove Street Cemetery is a living testament to New Haven's rich cultural heritage and the contributions of its residents to the development of the United States.

383.

The cemetery's board of directors includes representatives from Yale University, the New Haven Preservation Trust, and other organizations dedicated to its preservation.

384.

Grove Street Cemetery has been praised for its well-maintained grounds and efforts to balance preservation with modern needs.

385.

The cemetery is an excellent example of how historic sites can coexist within a bustling urban environment.

386.

The cemetery was one of the first cemeteries in the United States to offer perpetual care for grave sites.

387.

Several graves at Grove Street Cemetery are adorned with beautiful stained glass windows, adding to the artistic and cultural significance of the site.

388.

Many of the tombstones and monuments at the cemetery feature beautiful and poignant epitaphs, offering insights into the lives of those buried there.

389.

The cemetery was originally known as the "New Haven City Burial Ground" before it was officially named Grove Street Cemetery.

390.

The cemetery's proximity to Yale University makes it a popular destination for student groups and visitors interested in the history of the university and its founders.

391.

Grove Street Cemetery's beautiful architecture and serene ambiance have made it a popular location for weddings and other special events.

392.

The cemetery has been featured in numerous books and documentaries exploring its historical and cultural significance.

393.

Grove Street Cemetery has been recognized for its role in preserving the memory of individuals who played significant roles in shaping American history and culture.

394.

The cemetery is known for its strict guidelines on monument designs and placements to maintain its historical integrity.

395.

Several famous abolitionists, including Simeon Jocelyn and Josiah Willard Gibbs, are buried at Grove Street Cemetery.

396.

The cemetery has been a subject of interest for paranormal enthusiasts, with some claiming to have witnessed ghostly sightings and experiences.

397.

In 1821, the cemetery's board of directors adopted rules and regulations that prohibited burial of slaves and free Black people.

398.

The cemetery's architecture and landscaping reflect the early 19th-century shift in burial practices from crowded churchyards to more spacious and contemplative settings.

399.

Several notable figures associated with the early history of Yale University, such as the Reverend Timothy Dwight IV, are buried at Grove Street Cemetery.

400.

Grove Street Cemetery is not only a place of remembrance but also a celebration of the diverse individuals who contributed to the cultural and intellectual landscape of New Haven and the nation.

401.

The Green Cheeked Conure, also known as the Green Cheeked Parakeet, is a small parrot native to South America.

402.

They belong to the genus Pyrrhura and are part of the Psittacidae family, which includes other parrot species.

403.

Green Cheeked Conures are widely recognized for their playful and affectionate nature, making them popular as pets.

404.

They have a vibrant green body with a distinctive red patch on their lower back and blue feathers on their wings.

405.

The Green Cheeked Conure's head is predominantly gray with a bright green cheek patch, giving them their common name.

406.

In the wild, these conures inhabit the rainforests, woodlands, and savannahs of South America, particularly in countries like Brazil, Bolivia, and Argentina.

407.

Green Cheeked Conures are social birds and are often found in small flocks.

408.

They are known for their excellent mimicry abilities and can learn various sounds and phrases with training.

409.

Green Cheeked Conures have a high-pitched, piercing call that can be loud and may require some training to control.

410.

Their diet primarily consists of fruits, vegetables, seeds, and pellets.

411.

In captivity, a balanced diet is crucial to their overall health and well-being.

412.

Green Cheeked Conures are active and require ample space and mental stimulation to prevent boredom.

413.

They are curious birds and enjoy exploring their environment and playing with toys.

414.

As pets, they can be taught tricks and respond well to positive reinforcement training.

415.

Green Cheeked Conures have a life expectancy of about 10 to 20 years, depending on their diet, living conditions, and overall care.

416.

They are known for their acrobatic abilities and enjoy hanging upside down and playing with toys.

417.

Green Cheeked Conures are monogamous and form strong bonds with their chosen mate.

418.

They communicate with their flock using various vocalizations and body language.

419.

Breeding pairs of Green Cheeked Conures often build nests in tree cavities or hollows.

420.

Female Green Cheeked Conures typically lay a clutch of 4 to 6 eggs, which she incubates for about 23 to 26 days.

421.

Both parents actively participate in feeding and caring for the chicks after they hatch.

422.

Green Cheeked Conures are cavity-nesters and will often seek out nesting boxes or enclosed spaces for nesting in captivity.

423.

They are generally gentle and affectionate birds, making them suitable for families and individuals alike.

424.

In the wild, they are considered to be of least concern on the conservation status scale due to their stable populations.

425.

Green Cheeked Conures have an inquisitive and playful personality, which makes them delightful companions for owners who can provide them with attention and interaction.

426.

They are known for their ability to form strong bonds with their human caregivers and often enjoy spending time outside of their cage.

427.

Green Cheeked Conures are excellent climbers and love to explore their surroundings.

428.

They are naturally curious and enjoy investigating new toys and objects.

429.

These conures are known for their entertaining antics, such as hanging upside down and rolling on their backs.

430.

Green Cheeked Conures are intelligent birds and can quickly learn tricks and commands with positive reinforcement training.

431.

Some Green Cheeked Conures may learn to mimic human speech, although they are not as renowned for their talking abilities as some other parrot species.

432.

In the wild, their diet consists of various fruits, seeds, nuts, and berries.

433.

Green Cheeked Conures are known for their playful and clownish behavior, which endears them to their owners.

434.

They are active birds and require regular exercise to stay physically and mentally fit.

435.

Green Cheeked Conures have a strong beak, which they use to crack open seeds and nuts in the wild.

436.

Proper socialization from a young age is essential for Green Cheeked Conures to ensure they grow up to be well-adjusted and friendly pets.

437.

In some regions, Green Cheeked Conures are considered agricultural pests due to their fondness for raiding fruit crops.

438.

Green Cheeked Conures are crepuscular, meaning they are most active during dawn and dusk.

439.

They have a curious and exploratory nature, often poking and prodding at new objects in their environment.

440.

In captivity, Green Cheeked Conures should have plenty of toys and activities to keep them mentally stimulated.

441.

Green Cheeked Conures are generally good fliers and enjoy flying around their living space.

442.

They are susceptible to obesity if they are overfed or do not receive enough exercise.

443.

Green Cheeked Conures are known to enjoy taking baths, whether through a spray bottle or shallow water dish.

444.

These conures have a unique way of communicating their happiness and contentment, often making soft cooing sounds or even purring.

445.

They can be trained to step up on a hand or perch and are generally eager to interact with their owners.

446.

Green Cheeked Conures are monomorphic, meaning males and females look similar and can be challenging to sex without genetic testing or observing breeding behavior.

447.

They are social birds and can exhibit signs of distress if left alone for long periods.

448.

Green Cheeked Conures are susceptible to respiratory infections, so maintaining a clean living environment is crucial for their health.

449.

In the wild, they may form mixed-species flocks with other parrot species, which provides them with additional protection and social interactions.

450.

Green Cheeked Conures are delightful and charismatic companions, making them a popular choice for bird enthusiasts seeking an affectionate and playful pet bird.

451.

The Green Crab (Carcinus maenas) is a small to medium-sized crab species belonging to the family Portunidae.

452.

They are native to the Eastern Atlantic Ocean, ranging from northern Africa to Norway, but have become an invasive species in many parts of the world.

453.

Green Crabs have a characteristic greenish-brown color, with five distinct spines on each side of their carapace.

454.

They are well-known for their aggressive and opportunistic feeding behavior, preying on a wide variety of small marine organisms.

455.

Green Crabs are highly adaptable and can tolerate a range of environmental conditions, which contributes to their invasive success.

456.

The species is often associated with rocky shorelines, estuaries, and coastal marshes.

457.

Green Crabs are voracious omnivores and feed on algae, mollusks, crustaceans, small fish, and plant matter.

458.

They have strong claws that they use for both feeding and defense.

459.

Green Crabs are highly fecund, with females capable of producing up to 185,000 eggs per brood.

460.

Their reproductive rate and wide distribution contribute to their rapid population growth and invasive potential.

461.

Green Crabs have been introduced to various regions, including the East Coast of North America, the West Coast of North America, South America, Australia, and parts of Asia.

462.

As an invasive species, Green Crabs can outcompete and displace native crab species, negatively impacting local marine ecosystems.

463.

The introduction of Green Crabs to new areas is often attributed to ballast water exchange from ships or the aquaculture trade.

464.

Efforts to control Green Crab populations in invaded areas include trapping and culling, but complete eradication has proven challenging.

465.

The Green Crab has few natural predators in its non-native range, which contributes to its population growth.

466.

Green Crabs are known for their high tolerance to changes in salinity and temperature, allowing them to thrive in both brackish and temperate waters.

467.

They are agile and swift movers, with the ability to quickly escape predators and capture prey.

468.

Green Crabs can live for up to five years in the wild.

469.

Due to their aggressive nature and large numbers, they are considered a significant threat to economically valuable shellfish industries.

470.

Invasive Green Crabs have been implicated in the decline of native clam, oyster, and mussel populations.

471.

Despite their small size, Green Crabs are known for their fierce territorial disputes.

472.

Green Crabs have a complex social structure, with dominance hierarchies established through physical interactions.

473.

Their claws regenerate if lost due to predation or injury.

474.

Green Crabs are considered a delicacy in some culinary traditions, and efforts have been made to promote their use as a food source to help control their populations.

475.

The European Green Crab is a close relative of the invasive Green Crab and is native to the same regions in Europe.

476.

Green Crabs are highly adaptable to changes in their environment, allowing them to thrive in both natural and human-altered habitats.

477.

In regions where Green Crabs have invaded, they can have significant ecological impacts on seagrass beds and salt marsh habitats.

478.

Green Crabs have been implicated in the decline of native clam populations in New England, affecting local fisheries.

479.

The International Union for Conservation of Nature (IUCN) lists the Green Crab as one of the world's 100 worst invasive alien species.

480.

The invasive Green Crab is often referred to as a "super-invader" due to its ability to colonize and dominate new environments.

481.

Green Crabs have a specialized set of teeth in their stomachs that allow them to crush and grind food before digesting it.

482.

They have been found in a wide range of salinity levels, from fully marine waters to nearly freshwater environments.

483.

Green Crabs are known to burrow into sediment to seek refuge and avoid predation.

484.

In their native range, Green Crabs are an important part of the food chain, providing prey for larger predators.

485.

Their exoskeletons are used as a source of calcium for other organisms in the marine ecosystem.

486.

Green Crabs are capable of undergoing color changes to match their surroundings, providing camouflage and protection from predators.

487.

As an invasive species, Green Crabs are often targeted for eradication or control measures to protect native ecosystems.

488.

Efforts to mitigate their impact include the development of new fishing gear, the introduction of natural predators, and the promotion of alternative aquaculture practices.

489.

Green Crabs are believed to have been introduced to the West Coast of the United States in the mid-19th century.

490.

They are opportunistic scavengers and will eat almost anything they encounter, including carrion.

491.

Invasive Green Crabs have been reported to feed on eelgrass, which is a critical habitat for many marine species.

492.

Green Crabs are known for their exceptional sense of smell, which helps them locate food in the water.

493.

They have a unique mating behavior, with males attracting females through a series of courtship displays.

494.

In their native range, Green Crabs are an essential component of intertidal ecosystems, providing ecological balance and contributing to nutrient cycling.

495.

Green Crabs are considered "bioengineers" as they influence sediment dynamics and the structure of the habitats they inhabit.

496.

Their reproductive success is influenced by environmental factors, including water temperature and salinity.

497.

Green Crabs have been found to exhibit different behaviors and feeding habits in different regions, depending on the local ecosystem.

498.

They are known to dig burrows in soft sediment, providing shelter for themselves and other marine organisms.

499.

Green Crabs are highly adaptable to changes in food availability, which contributes to their success as an invasive species.

500.

Their invasiveness has prompted numerous scientific studies and management efforts to better understand and control their spread and impact on native ecosystems.

501.

The Hyatt hotel chain was founded by Jay Pritzker in 1957. The first hotel, Hyatt House, was opened near the Los Angeles International Airport.

502.

The name "Hyatt" was derived from the combination of Hyatt House and Hyatt Lodge, the first two hotels in the chain.

503.

The Hyatt Regency Atlanta, opened in 1967, was the first hotel to feature the distinctive atrium design, which has since become a hallmark of many Hyatt properties.

504.

Hyatt became the first hotel chain to introduce the concept of "resort hotels" in 1969, with the opening of Hyatt Regency Maui Resort & Spa in Hawaii.

505.

In 1972, Hyatt became the first hotel chain to offer an on-site fitness center for guests.

506.

The Grand Hyatt New York, opened in 1980, is notable for being the first hotel to feature a full-service Starbucks outlet.

507.

The first international Hyatt hotel, Hyatt Regency Hong Kong, opened in 1969.

508.

In 1980, Hyatt opened the Park Hyatt Tokyo, which gained international fame as one of the filming locations for the movie "Lost in Translation."

509.

Hyatt became a public company in 1979 and was listed on the New York Stock Exchange.

510.

The company expanded its portfolio with the acquisition of the Regency Hotel chain in 1980.

511.

The Hyatt Regency San Francisco, opened in 1973, was the first hotel in the world to feature a revolving rooftop restaurant.

512.

The iconic Hyatt Regency Chicago, opened in 1974, is one of the largest hotels in the world by room count.

513.

In 1994, Hyatt launched the loyalty program "Gold Passport," which was later rebranded as "World of Hyatt" in 2017.

514.

The Park Hyatt Sydney, opened in 1990, offers stunning views of the Sydney Opera House and Sydney Harbour Bridge.

515.

In 2011, Hyatt launched the Andaz brand, a boutique lifestyle hotel concept that offers unique, locally inspired experiences.

516.

The Hyatt Regency New Orleans, opened in 1976, became a temporary home for thousands of evacuees during Hurricane Katrina in 2005.

517.

Hyatt established its first hotel in India, the Hyatt Regency Delhi, in 1983.

518.

In 2014, Hyatt introduced the Hyatt Centric brand, catering to millennial travelers seeking authentic and local experiences.

519.

The Hyatt Regency Atlanta is known for hosting the annual Dragon Con convention, one of the largest multi-genre fan conventions in the United States.

520.

Hyatt acquired the luxury hotel brand Miraval Group in 2017, expanding its offerings in the wellness and spa industry.

521.

Hyatt has a strong commitment to sustainability and was recognized as one of the "World's Most Ethical Companies" by the Ethisphere Institute for multiple years.

522.

The Hyatt Regency Chicago has hosted numerous political events and conventions, including the 1996 Democratic National Convention.

523.

The Grand Hyatt Shanghai, opened in 1999, is one of the tallest hotels in the world and offers breathtaking views of the city skyline.

524.

The Hyatt Regency Orlando is one of the largest convention hotels in the United States, with over two million square feet of meeting space.

525.

The Hyatt Regency Lost Pines Resort & Spa, opened in 2006, is located on 405 acres of the Lost Pines Forest in Texas.

526.

In 2018, Hyatt acquired Two Roads Hospitality, adding several new brands to its portfolio, including Thompson Hotels and Joie de Vivre Hotels.

527.

Hyatt was one of the first hotel chains to implement a Global Care & Cleanliness Commitment in response to the COVID-19 pandemic.

528.

Hyatt has been recognized as one of the "100 Best Companies to Work For" by Fortune magazine for several years.

529.

The Hyatt Regency Sydney in Australia has the largest hotel rooftop in the city, offering panoramic views of Darling Harbour.

530.

In 2020, Hyatt opened its 1,000th hotel, the Alila Napa Valley in California.

531.

Hyatt Place hotels, launched in 2006, are designed for modern travelers seeking a seamless experience and comfortable accommodations.

532.

Hyatt operates the Hyatt Residence Club, a vacation ownership program with properties in desirable destinations.

533.

The Hyatt Regency Waikiki Beach Resort & Spa in Hawaii is located just steps away from the famous Waikiki Beach.

534.

Hyatt has been recognized as a leader in diversity and inclusion, receiving a perfect score on the Human Rights Campaign Corporate Equality Index.

535.

The Hyatt Regency Kyoto in Japan is designed to reflect the traditional architecture and serene ambiance of the historic city.

536.

In 2021, Hyatt announced plans to acquire Apple Leisure Group, a leading hospitality and leisure company.

537.

Hyatt is actively involved in community engagement and philanthropy through initiatives like Hyatt Thrive, supporting education and sustainability programs.

538.

The Hyatt Ziva and Hyatt Zilara brands offer all-inclusive resorts in popular vacation destinations.

539.

Hyatt Regency hotels are known for their convenient locations in city centers and near major airports.

540.

The Hyatt Regency Paris - Charles de Gaulle is the only hotel directly connected to Terminal 2 at Paris Charles de Gaulle Airport.

541.

The Hyatt House brand is designed for extended stay guests, offering residential-style accommodations and amenities.

<h1 style="text-align:center">542.</h1>

Hyatt operates the Exhale Spa brand, offering a holistic approach to wellness and mindfulness.

<h1 style="text-align:center">543.</h1>

The Hyatt Regency Tokyo is conveniently located in the Shinjuku district, one of Tokyo's major entertainment and business hubs.

<h1 style="text-align:center">544.</h1>

Hyatt hotels are known for their dedication to exceptional customer service and creating memorable guest experiences.

<h1 style="text-align:center">545.</h1>

The Hyatt Regency London - The Churchill is named after Sir Winston Churchill, who was a regular patron of the hotel.

<h1 style="text-align:center">546.</h1>

Hyatt's loyalty program, World of Hyatt, offers members exclusive benefits, rewards, and access to unique experiences.

<h1 style="text-align:center">547.</h1>

Hyatt hotels worldwide support local communities through initiatives like Hyatt's Good Taste Series, promoting sustainability and local ingredients.

<h1 style="text-align:center">548.</h1>

Hyatt Place hotels offer a Gallery Market, where guests can purchase snacks, beverages, and fresh meals 24/7.

<h1 style="text-align:center">549.</h1>

Hyatt's Global Head of Wellbeing is responsible for driving the company's commitment to well-being for guests and associates.

<h1 style="text-align:center">550.</h1>

The Hyatt Regency Atlanta celebrated its 50th anniversary in 2017, marking a significant milestone for the Hyatt brand and its history in the hospitality industry.

551.

The Hyatt Regency Atlanta celebrated its 50th anniversary in 2017, marking a significant milestone for the Hyatt brand and its history in the hospitality industry.

552.

The company was originally named Caterpillar Tractor Co. but later changed its name to Caterpillar Inc. in 1986.

553.

The iconic yellow color of Caterpillar equipment is officially known as "Caterpillar Yellow," and it is trademarked by the company.

554.

The Caterpillar logo, featuring the distinctive triangle and caterpillar track, was first introduced in 1931 and has remained largely unchanged ever since.

555.

Caterpillar's first product was the Caterpillar Twenty, a 2-ton tractor introduced in 1925.

556.

During World War II, Caterpillar was a major supplier of military equipment, including tanks, bulldozers, and other machinery.

557.

Caterpillar is known for its large bulldozers, and one of its most famous models is the D9, introduced in 1955.

558.

In 1948, Caterpillar became the first company to introduce a hydraulic track loader.

559.

The famous "Cat" name used by Caterpillar is derived from the abbreviation of the company's full name.

560.

Caterpillar equipment has been used in numerous high-profile construction projects, including the Hoover Dam and the Panama Canal expansion.

561.

In 1982, Caterpillar became the first company to manufacture a dozer with an elevated sprocket design, which improved machine balance and performance.

562.

The company introduced its first wheel loader, the 944, in 1959, marking its entry into the construction equipment market.

563.

Caterpillar's corporate headquarters is located in Deerfield, Illinois, USA.

564.

The company has a strong global presence, with manufacturing facilities and dealerships in more than 190 countries.

565.

Caterpillar is a Fortune 500 company and has consistently ranked among the largest corporations in the world by revenue.

566.

The Caterpillar Tractor Company acquired the rights to the "D4" designation from the U.S. Army after World War II, making it the first civilian tractor with that designation.

567.

In 1954, Caterpillar introduced its first motor grader, the No. 12, which became a popular machine for road construction and maintenance.

568.

Caterpillar's product line expanded over the years to include a wide range of construction equipment, mining machinery, and diesel engines.

569.

The company is a leading manufacturer of mining equipment, producing large mining trucks, excavators, and drilling machines.

570.

In 1985, Caterpillar introduced its first all-wheel drive loader, the 920.

571.

Caterpillar has a long history of innovation and has been granted numerous patents for its engineering designs and technologies.

572.

The company's large track-type tractors, also known as "dozers," have earned the nickname "Caterpillar Cats" due to their powerful capabilities.

573.

Caterpillar has been involved in the development of electric drive technology for its machines, reducing fuel consumption and emissions.

574.

The company has actively promoted sustainability and environmental responsibility in its operations and products.

575.

Caterpillar's diesel engines have been used in a wide range of applications, including marine vessels, locomotives, and power generation.

576.

The company's customers include construction companies, mining operations, agriculture, and various other industries requiring heavy machinery.

577.

The "Caterpillar Music" jingle, used in advertising campaigns, became a recognizable tune associated with the brand.

578.

Caterpillar is a major supplier to the U.S. military, providing equipment and support for various military operations.

579.

The company's manufacturing facilities use advanced technologies, including robotics and automation, to increase efficiency and productivity.

580.

Caterpillar has faced challenges in the past, including labor strikes and economic downturns, but has demonstrated resilience and adaptability.

581.

The Caterpillar Visitors Center, located in Peoria, Illinois, offers interactive exhibits and displays showcasing the company's history and products.

582.

Caterpillar has been involved in philanthropy, supporting various charitable organizations and community projects.

583.

The company has received numerous awards for its safety practices and commitment to employee well-being.

584.

Caterpillar's products have been used in disaster relief efforts, such as providing equipment for earthquake recovery and rebuilding after hurricanes.

585.

The company is known for its strong dealer network, providing sales, service, and support to customers around the world.

586.

Caterpillar has expanded its product offerings to include technology solutions, such as telematics and digital tools to enhance equipment performance and efficiency.

587.

The Caterpillar Foundation, established in 1952, focuses on initiatives related to education, basic human needs, and environmental sustainability.

588.

Caterpillar has been recognized as one of the "World's Most Admired Companies" by Fortune magazine.

589.

The company's Caterpillar Production System (CPS) is a comprehensive set of manufacturing principles and practices aimed at continuous improvement.

590.

The Caterpillar Global Mining headquarters is located in Tucson, Arizona, and is a center for mining equipment design and innovation.

591.

The Caterpillar Marine Center of Excellence, located in Hamburg, Germany, specializes in marine propulsion and power generation systems.

592.

In 1987, Caterpillar introduced its first skid steer loader, the 216.

593.

The company has a strong commitment to diversity and inclusion, striving to create an inclusive and equitable work environment.

594.

Caterpillar has been listed on the Dow Jones Sustainability Indices, recognizing its sustainability performance and practices.

595.

The Caterpillar Safety Services offers training and consultation to help organizations improve their safety culture and reduce workplace accidents.

596.

The company's financial services division, Caterpillar Financial Services Corporation (Cat Financial), provides financing solutions to customers worldwide.

597.

Caterpillar has a strong presence in the locomotive industry, producing diesel-electric locomotives for freight and passenger transport.

598.

The company has been recognized for its commitment to veterans and was named one of the "Best for Vets" employers by Military Times.

599.

Caterpillar actively engages in research and development to drive innovation and stay at the forefront of technology in the heavy machinery industry.

600.

The company's commitment to sustainability and social responsibility is reflected in its Environmental, Social, and Governance (ESG) reporting and initiatives.

601.

Hill-Stead was built between 1898 and 1901 for Alfred Atmore Pope and his family. It was designed by the renowned architect Theodate Pope Riddle, who was one of the first female architects in the United States.

602.

Theodate Pope Riddle designed Hill-Stead in the Colonial Revival style, with inspiration from 18th-century New England homes.

603.

The house sits on a 152-acre estate, which includes formal gardens, meadows, woodlands, and a pond.

604.

Hill-Stead is listed on the National Register of Historic Places and is a designated National Historic Landmark.

605.

The house features 33 rooms, including 19 bedrooms, 7 bathrooms, and 3 kitchens.

606.

Hill-Stead was equipped with modern amenities for its time, including central heating, electricity, and a dumbwaiter.

607.

The interior of the house is decorated with a collection of European and American art, including works by Monet, Manet, Whistler, and Cassatt.

608.

Hill-Stead's collection includes over 2,500 objects, ranging from paintings and decorative arts to textiles and manuscripts.

609.

The Hill-Stead collection was donated to the public in 1946 by Theodate Pope Riddle, who wanted to preserve her family home and share its beauty with the public.

610.

Hill-Stead became a museum in 1947, making it one of the first museums in the country to be opened to the public with the intent of sharing an intact collection.

611.

The estate's gardens were designed by landscape architect Warren H. Manning and include a sunken garden, a perennial garden, and a beautiful rose arbor.

612.

The estate also features a working farm that was once used for agriculture and horse breeding.

613.

Hill-Stead's sunken garden is one of the first of its kind in the United States and is inspired by the gardens of Europe.

614.

The house is renowned for its stunning views, overlooking the surrounding meadows and woodlands.

615.

Theodate Pope Riddle named the estate "Hill-Stead" because it sits on a hilltop overlooking the countryside.

616.

Hill-Stead's library contains over 2,000 volumes, including many rare and valuable books.

617.

The estate's art collection includes three paintings by Claude Monet, including his famous work "The Artist's Garden at Giverny."

618.

Hill-Stead's collection of Impressionist paintings is considered one of the finest in the United States.

619.

The museum offers guided tours of the house and gardens, allowing visitors to learn about the history of the estate and its art collection.

620.

Hill-Stead hosts various cultural events, including concerts, lectures, and art exhibitions.

621.

The estate was featured in the 1993 movie "The Age of Innocence," directed by Martin Scorsese and based on the novel by Edith Wharton.

622.

Hill-Stead's carriage house was converted into a museum shop and visitor center.

623.

Theodate Pope Riddle was an accomplished equestrian and was one of the first women to play polo in the United States.

624.

The estate's formal gardens were restored to their original design in the 1980s, based on archival photographs and plans.

625.

Hill-Stead's landscape was designed to mimic the English countryside, with meandering paths and picturesque views.

626.

The estate's collection includes a significant number of works by American artists, including Mary Cassatt, John Singer Sargent, and James McNeill Whistler.

627.

Hill-Stead's architecture and design have inspired many other homes and buildings in the Colonial Revival style.

628.

The museum offers educational programs for children and adults, including art classes and workshops.

629.

Hill-Stead hosts an annual Sunken Garden Poetry Festival, featuring readings by renowned poets in the beautiful sunken garden.

630.

The estate's iconic white fences and sweeping driveway create a picturesque and inviting entrance.

631.

Hill-Stead has been featured in various magazines and books as a prime example of American domestic architecture and design.

632.

The museum has a conservation lab on-site, where artworks and artifacts are carefully restored and preserved.

633.

Hill-Stead's collection includes Chinese porcelain, antique furniture, and rare books.

634.

The estate's collection of Japanese woodblock prints includes works by Hiroshige and Hokusai.

635.

Hill-Stead's formal gardens are meticulously maintained, and the estate is known for its beautiful seasonal displays.

636.

The museum offers special programs for schools and educational groups, including interactive tours and art-based activities.

637.

Hill-Stead is a popular venue for weddings, providing a beautiful backdrop for couples looking to tie the knot in a historic and elegant setting.

638.

The estate's main hall features a grand staircase, adorned with beautiful woodwork and ornate details.

639.

Hill-Stead's original 1901 lighting fixtures and Tiffany lamps are still in use, adding to the historic ambiance of the house.

640.

The estate's art collection is worth over $50 million and is considered one of the most significant private collections of its kind.

641.

Hill-Stead has been recognized by the American Association of Museums for its excellence in museum management and educational programs.

642.

Theodate Pope Riddle's architectural drawings and papers are preserved in the Library of Congress.

643.

The museum's gardens are maintained using sustainable and environmentally friendly practices.

644.

Hill-Stead offers docent-led tours in various languages, including Spanish and Mandarin, to accommodate international visitors.

645.

The museum has been the recipient of numerous awards and grants for its preservation efforts and educational initiatives.

646.

Hill-Stead is actively involved in community outreach and partners with local organizations to promote arts and culture in the region.

647.

The museum's grounds include walking trails that offer visitors the chance to explore the natural beauty of the estate.

648.

Hill-Stead participates in a wide range of cultural and educational events, including community festivals and celebrations.

649.

The museum has a strong commitment to accessibility and offers programs and services for visitors with disabilities.

650.

Hill-Stead is a cherished cultural and historical landmark in Connecticut and continues to attract visitors from around the world who come to appreciate its art, architecture, and natural beauty.

651.

The Samuel Huntington Birthplace was the childhood home of Samuel Huntington, who was born on July 16, 1731.

652.

Samuel Huntington was a prominent American political leader and one of the signers of the Declaration of Independence.

653.

The house was built in 1719 and is a well-preserved example of early New England architecture.

654.

The house is a two-and-a-half-story wood-frame structure with a central chimney and a saltbox roof.

655.

The house originally had four rooms on the first floor and two rooms on the second floor.

656.

The house was originally located in Windham, Connecticut, but was moved to Scotland, Connecticut, in 1953 to save it from demolition.

657.

The house was disassembled, moved, and reassembled at its current location in Scotland, Connecticut.

658.

The Samuel Huntington Birthplace was added to the National Register of Historic Places in 1970.

659.

The house is now owned and operated by the Governor Samuel Huntington Trust, a non-profit organization dedicated to preserving and interpreting the site.

660.

The house is furnished with period pieces and artifacts that provide a glimpse into colonial life in Connecticut.

661.

Visitors to the Samuel Huntington Birthplace can take guided tours of the house and learn about the life and times of Samuel Huntington.

662.

The house features a small gift shop where visitors can purchase books, souvenirs, and other items related to Samuel Huntington and colonial history.

663.

The Samuel Huntington Birthplace hosts special events and programs throughout the year, including historical reenactments, lectures, and workshops.

664.

The property surrounding the house includes a garden with historically accurate plants and herbs commonly grown during the colonial era.

665.

Samuel Huntington was a self-taught lawyer who practiced law in Connecticut before becoming involved in politics.

666.

Huntington served as the president of the Continental Congress from 1779 to 1781.

667.

Huntington was the 18th Governor of Connecticut, serving from 1786 to 1796.

668.

During his time as governor, Huntington oversaw the ratification of the United States Constitution by Connecticut in 1788.

669.

Huntington played a crucial role in the early years of the new nation, helping to shape its government and policies.

670.

He was one of the three delegates from Connecticut to sign the Declaration of Independence in 1776.

671.

Samuel Huntington's signature on the Declaration of Independence is the largest and most prominent.

672.

The Samuel Huntington Birthplace is one of the few remaining homes of a signer of the Declaration of Independence that is open to the public.

673.

The house is decorated with period furnishings, including antique furniture and household items.

674.

The Samuel Huntington Birthplace is a popular destination for school field trips and educational programs.

675.

The site offers interactive activities for children and families to learn about colonial life and the history of the United States.

676.

The Samuel Huntington Birthplace is open seasonally from May to October, with varying hours of operation.

677.

The property includes a barn and outbuildings, which add to the historical significance of the site.

678.

The birthplace is located in a quiet rural setting, surrounded by trees and fields.

679.

Samuel Huntington was known for his humility and commitment to public service.

680.

Huntington's father, Nathaniel Huntington, built the house and operated a tavern in the front room.

681.

The tavern served as a gathering place for travelers passing through the area.

682.

Samuel Huntington had eight siblings, and the large family lived in the house during his childhood.

683.

The house has been carefully restored and maintained to reflect its original appearance.

684.

The Samuel Huntington Birthplace is a significant historical site in Connecticut and is part of the state's rich colonial heritage.

685.

The site offers opportunities for visitors to engage with history through hands-on activities and interactive exhibits.

686.

The Governor Samuel Huntington Trust works to promote public awareness and appreciation of the life and accomplishments of Samuel Huntington.

687.

The Trust also operates educational programs for schools and community groups, both on-site and through outreach efforts.

688.

The Samuel Huntington Birthplace has been featured in various documentaries and publications about American history.

689.

The site provides a unique opportunity to explore the life and times of one of America's founding fathers in an authentic colonial setting.

690.

The house has been visited by numerous dignitaries and public figures, including presidents and members of Congress.

691.

The Samuel Huntington Birthplace is a testament to the importance of preserving and interpreting our nation's history for future generations.

692.

The site offers a tranquil and peaceful atmosphere, making it a serene destination for history enthusiasts and nature lovers alike.

693.

The Samuel Huntington Birthplace has become a symbol of national pride and a reminder of the sacrifices made by those who shaped the United States.

694.

The house and its grounds provide a picturesque backdrop for special events, such as weddings and private gatherings.

695.

The Governor Samuel Huntington Trust relies on donations and volunteer support to maintain and operate the site.

696.

The Samuel Huntington Birthplace is one of Connecticut's best-preserved examples of a colonial-era home.

697.

The Trust collaborates with other historical organizations and museums to promote awareness of Samuel Huntington and his legacy.

698.

The site offers an array of educational resources, including lesson plans and educational materials for teachers.

699.

The Samuel Huntington Birthplace welcomes visitors from all walks of life, providing a meaningful and enlightening experience for people of all ages.

700.

The Samuel Huntington Birthplace serves as a lasting tribute to a remarkable statesman and a vital chapter in the story of America's founding and growth as a nation.

701.

Green scarab beetles belong to the family Scarabaeidae, which includes thousands of species worldwide.

702.

The green scarab beetle is known for its vibrant metallic green color, which can vary slightly depending on the species.

703.

These beetles are commonly found in various habitats, including forests, grasslands, and gardens.

704.

Green scarab beetles play an essential role in the ecosystem as decomposers, helping to break down organic matter and recycle nutrients.

705.

In ancient Egyptian culture, scarab beetles were considered sacred and were associated with the sun god, Khepri, symbolizing renewal and rebirth.

706.

The green scarab beetle's exoskeleton is extremely hard and serves as a protective armor against predators.

707.

Adult green scarab beetles feed on fruits, leaves, and nectar, while the larvae feed on decaying plant material.

708.

Some green scarab beetles are attracted to light and may be found near outdoor light sources at night.

709.

These beetles are nocturnal, meaning they are active primarily during the night.

710.

Green scarab beetles communicate with each other through chemical signals, using pheromones to attract mates and mark territories.

711.

During mating, male green scarab beetles create buzzing sounds by rubbing their wings together.

712.

Females lay eggs in the soil, where the larvae will develop and feed on decaying organic matter.

713.

The larvae of green scarab beetles are known as grubs and have a C-shaped body with six legs.

714.

Grubs play an essential role in soil health by aerating the soil as they move and feed.

715.

Green scarab beetles are often associated with agricultural fields and may sometimes be considered pests, damaging crops and plants.

716.

In some cultures, green scarab beetles are believed to bring good luck and prosperity.

717.

The green scarab beetle's life cycle can take several months to a few years, depending on the species and environmental conditions.

718.

These beetles have specialized antennae that help them detect scents and locate food sources.

719.

Green scarab beetles are found on every continent except Antarctica.

720.

The species Phanaeus vindex is native to the southeastern United States and is known for its bright metallic green coloration.

721.

Green scarab beetles are capable of flying, although they may spend most of their time on the ground.

722.

Some species of green scarab beetles, such as the rose chafer (Cetonia aurata), are commonly seen in gardens and may be attracted to flowers.

723.

Green scarab beetles have a unique appearance that makes them stand out among other insects.

724.

Some species of green scarab beetles are known for their distinct patterns and markings on their exoskeleton.

725.

These beetles are often depicted in art and jewelry due to their beautiful and distinctive appearance.

726.

Green scarab beetles have been used as symbols in various cultures, representing aspects of life and spirituality.

727.

Some species of green scarab beetles are capable of rolling balls of dung, which they bury underground to use as a food source or to lay their eggs.

728.

Green scarab beetles have three pairs of legs and two pairs of wings.

729.

Some species of green scarab beetles are attracted to fermented fruit and may be found near fruit trees and vineyards.

730.

The green scarab beetle has a strong exoskeleton that helps protect it from predators and environmental stressors.

731.

The green color of these beetles is caused by a combination of pigments and structural properties of their exoskeleton.

732.

Green scarab beetles are relatively long-lived insects, with some species living for several months to a year or more.

733.

These beetles are cold-blooded, meaning their body temperature is regulated by the environment.

734.

The metallic green color of green scarab beetles is iridescent, meaning it changes in appearance depending on the angle of light.

735.

Some species of green scarab beetles are considered bioindicators, as their presence or absence can indicate the health of ecosystems.

736.

Green scarab beetles have chewing mouthparts, which they use to consume plant material.

737.

These beetles are often attracted to decaying fruits, flowers, and compost piles.

738.

The green scarab beetle is a favorite subject for insect collectors and entomologists due to its beauty and diversity.

739.

Some green scarab beetles are kept as pets in captivity by insect enthusiasts.

740.

Green scarab beetles have been depicted in ancient art and artifacts, dating back thousands of years.

741.

In some regions, green scarab beetles are believed to be symbols of fertility and prosperity.

742.

Some species of green scarab beetles are found at high altitudes in mountainous regions.

743.

Green scarab beetles have a varied diet, including fruits, leaves, flowers, and even small insects.

744.

The larvae of green scarab beetles are often found in the soil or decaying wood, where they feed on organic matter.

745.

Some species of green scarab beetles are attracted to light and may be seen flying around streetlights at night.

746.

The coloration of green scarab beetles can change with age, with some individuals becoming darker or lighter over time.

747.

Green scarab beetles are not harmful to humans and do not bite or sting.

748.

Some cultures believe that green scarab beetles bring messages from the spirit world and are considered to be messengers of the gods.

749.

The green scarab beetle is featured in various myths and legends, often representing transformation and renewal.

750.

The diversity and beauty of green scarab beetles make them a fascinating and important part of the natural world, worthy of admiration and protection.

751.

The green tree python (Morelia viridis) is a non-venomous snake species native to the rainforests of New Guinea, Indonesia, and Australia's Cape York Peninsula.

752.

Known for their vibrant green coloration, green tree pythons also come in various shades of yellow, blue, and turquoise.

753.

The green color of these snakes serves as excellent camouflage in their natural habitat, allowing them to blend seamlessly with the surrounding foliage.

754.

Green tree pythons have a prehensile tail, which means they can grasp and hold onto branches with it, aiding their arboreal lifestyle.

755.

They are often found coiled around tree branches, adopting a unique "S"-shape posture that helps them ambush prey and maintain stability.

756.

Unlike many other snake species, green tree pythons give birth to live young instead of laying eggs. This is known as viviparous reproduction.

757.

Female green tree pythons typically lay two eggs at a time, and these eggs incubate within her body until they hatch, resulting in the birth of fully formed neonates.

758.

Neonates (baby snakes) are often bright yellow or orange in color, with their green coloration developing as they mature.

759.

The average length of a green tree python ranges from 4 to 6 feet, with females usually being larger than males.

760.

Green tree pythons are constrictors, meaning they capture and kill their prey by coiling around them and squeezing until they can no longer breathe.

761.

Their diet primarily consists of small mammals, birds, and occasionally lizards.

762.

Green tree pythons are known for their calm demeanor and gentle nature, making them popular choices for reptile enthusiasts and collectors.

763.

These snakes have a triangular head with large eyes, providing them with excellent vision.

764.

Green tree pythons have heat-sensing pits on their upper and lower jaws, helping them detect warm-blooded prey.

765.

While their bites are non-venomous, green tree pythons have sharp teeth that can inflict painful wounds if provoked.

766.

Their skin has a unique pattern of scales, which creates a textured appearance when observed up close.

767.

Green tree pythons are known to shed their skin approximately every 4 to 8 weeks, a process called molting.

768.

Molting allows them to grow and replace old or damaged skin with a new layer.

769.

In captivity, green tree pythons require specific care, including maintaining high humidity levels and providing branches for climbing.

770.

They are primarily arboreal, spending most of their time in trees, and are not as comfortable on the ground.

771.

Green tree pythons are solitary animals, and adult individuals usually prefer to stay alone in their territory.

772.

Males have longer and more slender bodies compared to females, which is an adaptation for finding and gripping females during mating.

773.

Breeding in green tree pythons typically occurs during the wet season when food availability is higher.

774.

The green tree python's scientific name, Morelia viridis, is derived from the Italian naturalist Andrea Cesalpino and refers to its green color.

775.

The International Union for Conservation of Nature (IUCN) classifies green tree pythons as a species of "Least Concern," as they are not currently facing significant threats in the wild.

776.

Green tree pythons are popular subjects for photographers and artists due to their striking appearance.

777.

In the wild, green tree pythons play a crucial role in controlling the populations of their prey species, helping to maintain a balanced ecosystem.

778.

Their green coloration is not just for camouflage; it also helps them regulate their body temperature by absorbing sunlight.

779.

When threatened, green tree pythons may flatten their bodies, displaying their vivid colors and creating an intimidating appearance.

780.

Despite their striking appearance, these snakes are generally not aggressive toward humans and tend to retreat when confronted.

781.

Green tree pythons have excellent muscle control, allowing them to move gracefully through the treetops.

782.

They possess a specialized jaw structure that enables them to open their mouths wide enough to consume prey larger than their heads.

783.

In captivity, green tree pythons require specific UVB lighting to maintain their health and proper calcium absorption.

784.

Their lifespan in the wild is estimated to be around 10 to 20 years, while in captivity, with proper care, they can live up to 20-30 years.

785.

Green tree pythons are sometimes kept as pets, but potential owners should research their care requirements thoroughly before getting one.

786.

In certain cultures, green tree pythons are considered sacred animals and are revered in local myths and beliefs.

787.

Their natural habitat is threatened by deforestation due to logging and agriculture, leading to habitat loss for this species.

788.

Green tree pythons are excellent swimmers and are known to cross rivers and streams in search of food.

789.

These snakes have a slow metabolism, which allows them to go for extended periods without eating.

790.

Green tree pythons have been observed hanging upside-down from branches, using their strong tails to hold onto the tree while hunting or resting.

791.

The coloration of green tree pythons can change slightly depending on factors such as temperature, humidity, and lighting.

792.

In their natural habitat, green tree pythons may face predation from birds of prey and larger snakes.

793.

While green tree pythons are not the largest snake species, their stunning appearance and unique behaviors make them popular attractions in zoos and wildlife parks.

794.

These snakes have a relatively slow growth rate, especially during the early stages of their life.

795.

Green tree pythons have evolved to have excellent gripping capabilities, thanks to their unique belly scales that allow them to anchor themselves to surfaces.

796.

They are sometimes kept in captivity for educational purposes, helping people learn about the importance of conserving their natural habitat.

797.

Green tree pythons are a part of the complex and diverse ecosystem of rainforests, contributing to the overall biodiversity of their habitat.

798.

Green tree pythons are known to have different color phases in different regions, reflecting the diversity within their species.

799.

The conservation of green tree pythons involves preserving their habitats, enforcing laws against illegal pet trade, and raising awareness about their ecological significance.

800.

Green tree pythons are a remarkable example of nature's intricate designs, demonstrating the beauty and adaptations that come with living in the canopy of rainforests.

801.

WebMD was founded in 1996 by Jeff Arnold and James H. Clark with the goal of providing health information to the public in an easily accessible online format.

802.

The company's original name was "Healthscape," but it later changed to WebMD in 1999 to better reflect its online presence and focus.

803.

WebMD's initial mission was to create a reliable and comprehensive source of medical information to empower individuals to make informed health decisions.

804.

WebMD went public in 1999 and quickly became one of the most visited health websites on the internet.

805.

The website's comprehensive medical content covers a wide range of topics, from general health and wellness to specific medical conditions, treatments, medications, and more.

806.

WebMD offers tools such as symptom checkers, interactive health assessments, and personalized health recommendations based on user inputs.

807.

The site also provides expert-reviewed articles, news stories, and videos about health-related issues.

808.

In the early 2000s, WebMD faced criticism for perceived conflicts of interest due to its partnerships with pharmaceutical companies, which raised concerns about the neutrality of its content.

809.

Despite criticism, WebMD continued to expand its offerings, including the addition of discussion forums where users could share their health experiences and seek advice from peers.

810.

In 2008, WebMD acquired the online community Medscape, which provides information and resources for healthcare professionals.

811.

WebMD has won several awards for its user-friendly design and its contributions to improving health literacy.

812.

The website has been visited by millions of people worldwide, making it one of the most popular health-related websites on the internet.

813.

WebMD offers mobile apps for both iOS and Android devices, allowing users to access health information on the go.

814.

The company expanded its offerings to include a variety of health tools, such as calorie counters, exercise trackers, and medication reminders.

815.

WebMD's success attracted the attention of multiple investors and partners, leading to its acquisition by HLTH Corporation in 1999.

816.

In 2010, WebMD Health Corp. was created as a separate entity when it was spun off from HLTH Corporation.

817.

The company faced controversies over time, including criticism for symptom checkers that sometimes provided inaccurate or alarming information.

818.

WebMD has partnered with healthcare providers and organizations to offer information on clinical trials, allowing users to learn about potential treatment options.

819.

The company has also delved into telehealth services, providing users with the ability to consult with medical professionals remotely.

820.

WebMD launched its "Health Services" division, which offers wellness programs and resources to employers and health insurance companies.

821.

WebMD Magazine, a print publication, was introduced to provide readers with health-related articles and features.

822.

In 2012, WebMD launched its Medscape app, offering medical professionals access to clinical information, research, and educational resources.

823.

The WebMD Foundation was established to promote health education and support initiatives to improve public health awareness.

824.

Over the years, WebMD has received various awards for its contributions to health communication and education.

825.

The company has been recognized for its efforts to provide accurate and up-to-date medical information to the public.

826.

WebMD has been involved in numerous public health campaigns, providing resources and information about various health issues.

827.

WebMD's strong online presence has made it a go-to resource for individuals seeking health information before, during, and after medical appointments.

828.

The website has undergone several redesigns and updates to improve user experience and accessibility.

829.

WebMD has a team of medical experts, including doctors, nurses, and other healthcare professionals, who review and validate the accuracy of the content.

830.

In recent years, WebMD has expanded its content to include information about mental health, fitness, nutrition, and alternative therapies.

831.

The website has also become a platform for sharing personal health stories and experiences, allowing users to connect with others facing similar challenges.

832.

WebMD's quizzes and self-assessment tools have gained popularity among users interested in learning more about their health habits and risks.

833.

The company has embraced social media platforms, sharing health tips, news, and educational content to engage with its audience.

834.

WebMD has played a role in raising awareness about health-related issues, such as the opioid epidemic and mental health stigmas.

835.

The website's credibility and reliability have led it to be referenced by healthcare professionals and educators.

836.

WebMD's influence on the digital health landscape has inspired the creation of similar health information platforms and apps.

837.

The company has been praised for its role in helping patients better understand medical conditions and treatment options.

838.

In response to misinformation and fake news related to health, WebMD has actively worked to provide evidence-based information.

839.

WebMD has developed partnerships with medical schools, hospitals, and research institutions to ensure that its content is accurate and up-to-date.

840.

The company's commitment to health education led to the establishment of the "WebMD Health Hero Awards," recognizing individuals who have made significant contributions to public health.

841.

Over the years, WebMD's content has evolved to address changing health trends and emerging health concerns.

842.

WebMD has contributed to the growth of eHealth, providing a model for other health websites and apps.

843.

The website's design and user interface have been praised for their simplicity and ease of navigation.

844.

WebMD has been recognized for its efforts to provide information in a format that is accessible to individuals with disabilities.

845.

The company's focus on evidence-based health information aligns with the broader movement toward increasing health literacy.

846.

WebMD's engagement with medical professionals and experts has led to collaborations on articles and educational materials.

847.

The website has offered specialized content for specific demographics, such as women's health and parenting.

848.

WebMD's mobile apps have allowed users to access health information and resources wherever they are.

849.

The company has played a role in fostering conversations about health and wellness through its online communities and forums.

850.

WebMD's history reflects its ongoing commitment to providing accurate, reliable, and accessible health information to empower individuals to make informed decisions about their well-being.

851.

Oracle Corporation was founded in 1977 by Larry Ellison, Bob Miner, and Ed Oates. The company's original name was Software Development Laboratories (SDL).

852.

The company's flagship product, the Oracle Database, was initially developed as a project for the CIA. It was named after a project code-named "Oracle."

853.

Oracle's first commercial database, Oracle Version 2, was released in 1979, introducing the concepts of relational database management systems (RDBMS) to the industry.

854.

The company changed its name to "Relational Software, Inc." in 1982 and then to "Oracle Corporation" in 1983 to better reflect its primary product.

855.

Oracle's relational database technology revolutionized the way data was stored and retrieved, providing a more structured and efficient approach compared to traditional flat-file databases.

856.

In the 1980s, Oracle pioneered the concept of the "Oracle Certified Professional" (OCP) certification, offering professionals a way to validate their expertise in Oracle technologies.

857.

Oracle released the first version of its application server in 1995, expanding its offerings beyond databases to include middleware and enterprise software.

858.

The company's growth was fueled by its focus on providing comprehensive software solutions for businesses, including customer relationship management (CRM), enterprise resource planning (ERP), and more.

859.

Oracle went public in 1986, becoming one of the first major software companies to be listed on the NASDAQ stock exchange.

860.

In 1990, Oracle released its first version of the Oracle Applications suite, which included modules for financials, human resources, and manufacturing.

861.

Oracle made several strategic acquisitions throughout its history, including the acquisition of PeopleSoft in 2005 and Sun Microsystems in 2010, which provided hardware and software components.

862.

Oracle introduced its own version of the Java programming language, known as Oracle Java, after acquiring Sun Microsystems, which was a significant player in the Java development community.

863.

Oracle's database technology became a cornerstone of many enterprise applications and systems worldwide, powering critical business processes.

864.

The company is known for its focus on database security, offering features like data encryption, auditing, and access controls to protect sensitive information.

865.

Oracle became a leader in cloud computing, offering a range of cloud services including database as a service (DBaaS), infrastructure as a service (IaaS), and software as a service (SaaS).

866.

Oracle's acquisitions extended to the realm of cloud services, with the purchase of cloud computing companies like NetSuite and RightNow Technologies.

867.

Oracle's annual OpenWorld conference became one of the largest technology conferences, attracting thousands of attendees to learn about the company's products, services, and vision.

868.

Larry Ellison, one of the co-founders, served as the company's CEO for many years and played a pivotal role in shaping Oracle's strategy and direction.

869.

Oracle's acquisition of BEA Systems in 2008 solidified its position in the middleware market and strengthened its offerings in the application server space.

870.

The company's "Oracle Academy" program offers educational institutions resources and curriculum to teach students about database technology and computer science.

871.

Oracle's products have been used in various industries, including finance, healthcare, telecommunications, and government.

872.

The company's business model shifted from primarily selling software licenses to offering cloud-based subscriptions and services to adapt to changing industry trends.

873.

Oracle has a significant presence in Silicon Valley, with its headquarters located in Redwood City, California.

874.

The company has received numerous awards for its innovation, including being named to Fortune magazine's list of "World's Most Admired Companies."

875.

Oracle's Java programming language continues to be widely used for developing a variety of applications, from mobile apps to enterprise software.

876.

Oracle's focus on business applications has led to the development of industry-specific solutions, such as healthcare, retail, and manufacturing software.

877.

The company's commitment to research and development has led to the creation of cutting-edge technologies, including advancements in artificial intelligence and machine learning.

878.

Oracle has established a strong global presence, with offices and operations in countries around the world.

879.

The Oracle Cloud Infrastructure offers a scalable and secure platform for businesses to run their applications and services in the cloud.

880.

The company's cloud offerings include database services, analytics, artificial intelligence, internet of things (IoT), and more.

881.

Oracle has embraced open-source technologies and contributed to various open-source projects, including the MySQL database management system.

882.

The company's corporate culture emphasizes innovation, teamwork, and diversity in its workforce.

883.

Oracle has been involved in various philanthropic initiatives, supporting education, disaster relief efforts, and other social causes.

884.

The company's commitment to sustainability includes efforts to reduce its carbon footprint and promote environmentally friendly practices.

885.

Oracle's acquisition of NetSuite helped expand its cloud-based ERP offerings and strengthened its presence in the mid-market segment.

886.

The company's annual revenue and market capitalization place it among the largest technology companies in the world.

887.

Oracle's comprehensive suite of tools for developers includes integrated development environments (IDEs) and tools for database management and application deployment.

888.

The company's database technology is known for its scalability, reliability, and performance, making it a popular choice for mission-critical applications.

889.

Oracle's Autonomous Database, powered by artificial intelligence and machine learning, can self-tune, self-patch, and self-secure, reducing manual maintenance efforts.

890.

The company's focus on cloud computing aligns with industry trends and the growing demand for scalable and flexible IT solutions.

891.

Oracle has a strong presence in the business analytics and data visualization space, offering tools for data exploration and insights.

892.

The company's solutions have helped organizations streamline their operations, improve customer experiences, and make data-driven decisions.

893.

Oracle's customer base includes a wide range of companies, from startups to Fortune 500 enterprises.

894.

Oracle's acquisition of Sun Microsystems enabled it to offer a full technology stack, from hardware to software, to provide end-to-end solutions.

895.

The company's leadership in database technology has earned it a reputation for data management excellence.

896.

Oracle Cloud Marketplace provides customers with a platform to discover, deploy, and manage a variety of cloud applications and services.

897.

Oracle has been recognized for its commitment to diversity and inclusion in the workplace.

898.

The company's partnerships with other technology leaders and startups have contributed to its ecosystem of products and services.

899.

Oracle's involvement in the Java community has led to its participation in shaping the future direction of the language.

900.

As technology continues to evolve, Oracle remains a significant player in the software industry, adapting its offerings to meet the changing needs of businesses and organizations worldwide.

901.

The Philip Johnson Glass House is a renowned architectural masterpiece located in New Canaan, Connecticut, USA.

902.

The Glass House was designed by architect Philip Johnson, and it is considered one of his most iconic and influential works.

903.

The Glass House was completed in 1949 and served as Philip Johnson's personal residence for over five decades.

904.

The Glass House is a prime example of the International Style of architecture, characterized by its minimalist design, use of glass, and integration with nature.

905.

The house consists of a single rectangular glass-walled pavilion with no interior walls, creating an open and seamless living space.

906.

The Glass House's design was inspired by the work of architect Ludwig Mies van der Rohe, particularly his Farnsworth House.

907.

The Glass House's transparency blurs the boundaries between the interior and exterior, allowing for an immersive connection with the surrounding landscape.

908.

The property also features several other structures, including the Brick House, Da Monsta, Ghost House, Sculpture Gallery, and Library/Study.

909.

The Glass House is situated on a 49-acre estate that includes gardens, meadows, woods, and a man-made pond.

910.

The Glass House has been designated a National Historic Landmark and is recognized as one of the most important architectural landmarks in the United States.

911.

The Glass House is part of the National Trust for Historic Preservation's Historic Artists' Homes and Studios program.

912.

The Glass House and its surrounding structures showcase Johnson's evolving design aesthetic over several decades.

913.

The Glass House became a place for artistic gatherings and intellectual discussions, hosting influential figures from the worlds of art, architecture, and design.

914.

The Glass House's minimalist design influenced a generation of architects and designers who admired its simplicity and integration with nature.

915.

The Glass House was featured on the cover of Time magazine in 1953, bringing attention to Johnson's innovative approach to architecture.

916.

The Glass House features radiant heating embedded in the concrete floor, a cutting-edge technology for its time.

917.

The property's Brick House was designed as a guest house and includes a more traditional architectural style compared to the Glass House.

918.

Johnson's design philosophy for the Glass House was "each building must be true to itself, logically and architecturally."

919.

The Glass House's location was carefully chosen to take advantage of views of the surrounding landscape and changing seasons.

920.

The estate includes several sculptures and art installations, creating a dynamic interplay between architecture and art.

921.

Philip Johnson donated the Glass House and its surrounding property to the National Trust for Historic Preservation in 1986.

922.

The Glass House was opened to the public as a museum in 2007, allowing visitors to experience Johnson's innovative architectural vision firsthand.

923.

Tours of the Glass House and the surrounding structures provide insight into Johnson's design principles and his impact on modern architecture.

924.

The site hosts educational programs, lectures, and events that explore the intersection of architecture, design, and culture.

925.

The Glass House is known for its harmony with nature, with Johnson once describing it as "a totally transparent house... like living in a tree."

926.

The Glass House's transparency allowed Johnson to enjoy panoramic views of the changing seasons and the changing colors of the landscape.

927.

The Glass House has inspired many contemporary architects and designers to experiment with transparent and open designs.

928.

The Glass House's innovative use of glass panels for walls and roofing influenced the development of modern building materials and construction methods.

929.

The Glass House's design is emblematic of Johnson's belief in the power of architecture to influence human experience and perception.

930.

The site's Brick House is a departure from the Glass House's transparency, showcasing Johnson's versatility and willingness to experiment.

931.

Johnson's use of glass in the design of the Glass House challenged conventional notions of privacy and shelter.

932.

The Glass House's minimalist design philosophy reflects Johnson's belief that architecture should evoke an emotional response in its occupants.

933.

The Glass House's site-specific design highlights the importance of context in architecture, as the building interacts with its surroundings in unique ways.

934.

The Glass House's interior was sparsely furnished, with iconic pieces of modern furniture that complemented its architectural aesthetic.

935.

The site's Sculpture Gallery features rotating exhibitions of contemporary art, continuing Johnson's tradition of integrating art and architecture.

936.

The Glass House's impact extends beyond the field of architecture, influencing disciplines such as art, design, and philosophy.

937.

The Glass House's open design challenged traditional ideas of domesticity and privacy, sparking discussions about the role of architecture in modern society.

938.

The Glass House's landscaping was carefully designed to create a harmonious blend of nature and architecture, enhancing the visitor's experience.

939.

The property's structures are interconnected through pathways and landscaped areas, encouraging exploration and discovery.

940.

The Glass House's innovative design elements, such as its sliding doors and minimalist interiors, have been replicated and emulated in subsequent architectural projects.

941.

The Glass House's simplicity and transparency make it a canvas for the changing qualities of light, shadow, and reflection throughout the day.

942.

The Glass House's architectural legacy is not only in its physical design but also in the conversations and ideas it has generated over the years.

943.

The Glass House embodies Johnson's fascination with architectural experimentation and his desire to push the boundaries of conventional design.

944.

The Glass House's interior layout emphasizes the importance of spatial flow and circulation, with movable furniture allowing for flexible use.

945.

The Glass House's design exemplifies Johnson's belief that architecture should engage with its natural surroundings and foster a deep connection to the environment.

946.

The Glass House's architectural significance extends beyond its physical form, encompassing its historical context and the ideas it represents.

947.

The Glass House's integration with nature extends to its roof, which appears to float above the glass walls, blurring the distinction between interior and exterior.

948.

The Glass House's design philosophy is rooted in the belief that architecture can shape human experience and create spaces that resonate emotionally.

949.

The Glass House is a testament to Johnson's ability to synthesize artistic, cultural, and technological influences into a cohesive architectural vision.

950.

The Glass House continues to inspire architects, designers, and enthusiasts worldwide, serving as a living testament to the enduring impact of innovative design on culture and society.

951.

The Kimberly Mansion was built in 1882 by John R. Kimberly, one of the founders of the Kimberly-Clark Corporation.

952.

The mansion was designed by renowned architect William Waters, who also designed several other notable buildings in the Neenah area.

953.

The Kimberly Mansion is a prime example of the Victorian Gothic architectural style, characterized by its ornate detailing and steeply pitched roofs.

954.

The mansion's architecture features intricate woodwork, pointed arches, and decorative elements commonly associated with the Gothic Revival style.

955.

The mansion is situated on a large estate overlooking Lake Winnebago, offering breathtaking views of the water.

956.

The Kimberly Mansion is listed on the National Register of Historic Places, recognizing its architectural and historical significance.

957.

The mansion was originally built as a summer residence for the Kimberly family, who were prominent figures in the paper industry.

958.

The Kimberly family played a significant role in the growth of Neenah, contributing to the establishment of schools, churches, and public services.

959.

The mansion's interior features exquisite detailing, including intricate wood carvings, stained glass windows, and decorative moldings.

960.

The mansion boasts over 11,000 square feet of living space, providing ample room for the family's activities and entertainment.

961.

The Kimberly Mansion is known for its turret, a characteristic feature of Gothic Revival architecture, which adds to the mansion's unique appearance.

962.

The mansion's grounds were meticulously landscaped, featuring gardens, terraced lawns, and pathways.

963.

The mansion's construction materials included locally sourced limestone, adding to its architectural integrity.

964.

The Kimberly family entertained guests from across the country in the mansion's grand spaces, hosting social events and gatherings.

965.

The mansion's interior is adorned with period furnishings, showcasing the lifestyle and tastes of the late 19th century.

966.

The mansion's design and architecture reflect the wealth and success of the Kimberly family, who were prominent industrialists.

967.

The Kimberly Mansion has undergone preservation efforts to maintain its original charm and architectural features.

968.

The mansion's exterior and interior detailing are a testament to the craftsmanship of the artisans and craftsmen who worked on its construction.

969.

The mansion's location on Lake Winnebago made it an ideal summer retreat, offering a cool breeze and scenic views.

970.

The mansion's expansive verandas and porches provided comfortable spaces for relaxation and enjoying the outdoors.

971.

The Kimberly Mansion is an example of how wealthy families in the late 19th century showcased their social status through opulent homes.

972.

The mansion's design incorporates both functional and aesthetic elements, blending form and function seamlessly.

973.

The Kimberly Mansion is a symbol of the paper industry's importance to Neenah's growth and development.

974.

The mansion's grounds include mature trees, creating a picturesque setting that complements the architecture.

975.

The Kimberly Mansion's prominent location on a hill overlooking the lake made it a focal point of the landscape.

976.

The mansion's windows are designed with intricate stained glass panels, adding a touch of color and elegance to the interior.

977.

The mansion's interior features high ceilings and spacious rooms, enhancing its grandeur and sense of scale.

978.

The Kimberly Mansion has been recognized for its architectural significance by local preservation organizations.

979.

The mansion's historical tours offer visitors a glimpse into the lifestyles of affluent families during the late 19th century.

980.

The Kimberly family's legacy extends beyond the mansion, as they were philanthropists who contributed to the betterment of the Neenah community.

981.

The mansion's location near the water allowed for water-based recreational activities, making it a desirable summer destination.

982.

The Kimberly Mansion's architectural style reflects the romanticism and fascination with the past that characterized the Victorian era.

983.

The mansion's exterior features ornate woodwork and detailing, showcasing the craftsmanship of the era.

984.

The mansion's design was influenced by the Aesthetic Movement, which emphasized artistic and decorative qualities in architecture and design.

985.

The Kimberly Mansion's gardens were designed to complement the mansion's architecture, creating a cohesive and harmonious environment.

986.

The mansion's historical significance extends beyond its architecture, as it tells the story of the Kimberly family's contributions to industry and society.

987.

The Kimberly Mansion serves as a reminder of Neenah's history as a hub of industrial innovation and development.

988.

The mansion's proximity to the Kimberly-Clark Corporation's headquarters underscores the connection between the family and their business ventures.

989.

The mansion's design incorporates elements from various architectural styles, reflecting the eclectic tastes of the era.

990.

The Kimberly Mansion has been featured in architectural and historical publications, highlighting its significance in the region.

991.

The mansion's original furnishings and décor reflect the elegance and opulence of the Victorian era.

992.

The Kimberly Mansion's architecture stands as a representation of the family's prominence in both local and national contexts.

993.

The mansion's location on the lakefront allowed the Kimberly family to enjoy boating and water-based leisure activities.

994.

The mansion's architectural details, such as its pointed arches and decorative finials, exemplify the characteristics of the Gothic Revival style.

995.

The Kimberly Mansion's architectural influence can be seen in the design of other structures in the Neenah area.

996.

The mansion's historical significance has led to its preservation and recognition as a cultural landmark.

997.

The Kimberly Mansion's historical tours provide visitors with insights into the life of the Kimberly family and the era in which they lived.

998.

The mansion's architecture represents a fusion of traditional elements with contemporary design ideas of the late 19th century.

999.

The Kimberly Mansion's enduring presence in Neenah's landscape speaks to its lasting impact on the community and its history.

1000.

The mansion's architectural details, both interior and exterior, continue to capture the imagination of visitors interested in the history of Neenah and the Kimberly family.